"WHEN I
SIXTY-FOU..

1001 THINGS TO DO AT 60+

Chris Foote Wood

www.capallbann.co.uk

"WHEN I'M SIXTY-FOUR"

1001 THINGS TO DO AT 60+

©Copyright Chris Foote Wood 2007

ISBN 186163 2894
ISBN 13 9781861632890

British Library Cataloguing in Publication Data
A catalogue for this book is available from the British Library

Cover design by HR Design

Published by:

Capall Bann Publishing
Auton Farm
Milverton
Somerset
TA4 1NE

for Frances

"Will you still need me
Will you still feed me
When I'm Sixty-Four?"
- Beatles song

Cover picture: Chris Foote Wood in foreign parts

Contents

INTRODUCTION

It's not the years in your life that count, it's the life in your years.

Fact: anyone reaching the age of sixty nowadays can look forward to at least two more decades of active life. That's twenty years. The question is, what are you going to do with those twenty or more extra, precious years?

"I'm going to put my feet up," I hear you say. Wrong. That's the worst thing you can do. Take time off to relax, by all means. But "relaxing" and doing nothing else is a recipe for an early grave. Do you need to keep on working full time? Not unless you really want to, but why not have the best of both worlds? Take plenty of time to relax and enjoy yourself, but also make the time to continue with some vital activity, whether paid or unpaid, that engages your hand and brain on a daily basis. Being active and involved is the secret to keeping yourself fit and healthy and truly enjoying those extra decades of life that improving living standards and health care have given us.

Time was when the "average" man retired at sixty-five, moving abruptly from full-time work to doing nothing, before dying at sixty-eight. Three years of retirement? Now it's more likely to be thirty or forty. Anyway, let's forget about retirement in the traditional sense. Right now, the government is thinking of abolishing the age of retirement. And a good thing too. Not that I'm advocating we all work till we drop (although I intend to). Exactly when you formally leave the workplace, at fifty, sixty or seventy, doesn't matter. What matters is that we make the most of our brains and bodies for all our lives, and not stop doing so at some arbitrary age limit or when we leave full-time work.

We are all different. So the general layout of this book is to throw out an idea, toss it around, look at all the ramifications, and come up with a few, hopefully helpful, suggestions. The rest is up to you. Take from this book the bits that suit you, and ignore the rest. Hopefully there'll be enough good bits to compensate for the useless rubbish of the remainder.

I hope this book will inspire you to make the most of all of your life, but most especially in the golden years God, nature and/or the National Health Service have given us. The days of having a career, just one career, in your working life are over. I started my third career at the age of sixty-three. Future generations will have several careers. Remember, retirement should be a process, not an event. So, go to it. Get those brains and bodies working. And live happier, healthier – and longer!

Chris Foote Wood
Bishop Auckland
County Durham
Email: chris@northernwriters.co.uk
Web: www.northernwriters.co.uk
April 2007

Turned Sixty in '06: Bill Clinton, George W Bush, Liza Minelli, Steven Spielberg, Oliver Stone, Jack Straw, Joanna Lumley, Timothy Dalton, Dolly Parton, Diane Keaton, Tommy Lee Jones, Donald Trump, Cher, Felicity Kendal, Susan Saradon, Alan Rickman, Marianne Faithful [1].

Chapter One

DO IT NOW!

Don't wait until it's too late

I started this book on my sixty-fourth birthday. Really, I should have begun it on my sixty-third birthday, a year before, or even earlier. I've called this book "*When I'm Sixty-Four*" – all too obviously, a line from a Beatles song – really it should be called "Do It Now." Yes. "Do it now." Or even sooner.

The fact is, I'm puzzled about my age and the ageing process. Both are happening to me, but not in the way that I thought. I certainly don't think of myself as being "old". In fact, I'm still waiting for middle age to appear! While I accept I have become slower as the years go by, I certainly don't feel old. Nor (I flatter myself) do I actually look old. Well, not that old anyway. I have a photo of my Grandad and me when I was about eight years old. That would make him about sixty, younger than I am today. Yet my Grandad, who I loved dearly, looks a really, really old man.

To be fair, when I was eight, Grandad (this was my father's father, as my mother's father died when I was a baby) had already been through the First World War. He fought in Palestine, at the Dardanelles and on the Western Front. Hewent through the twenties and the thirties and the Second World War. Then he had all the problems after world war two with austerity, rationing and so on. No wonder he looked old!

Likewise, my dear old Dad was a child in the twenties and a young man in the thirties. He fought in the second world war, came through rationing and austerity, and struggled to earn a living for himself, his wife (my mother), me and my three sisters. In addition, he became a very successful writer - in his spare time. He didn't look too great towards the end of his life, but he had been ill for quite some time when he died at the age of eighty-one. But Dad still kept something of his roguish charm that always wowed the ladies, even in his later years.

As for me, I reckon I had a pretty good time of it. Although I was a "war baby", I was much too young to be affected by WW2. I do remember Plymouth being bombed, but that was just a great adventure to me. Yes, there was the wartime diet, but as it turned out it was the best possible diet, extremely healthy and what I am sure has laid the foundation for my relatively good health in my relatively older years. Looked at from a health point of view, rationing was a damn good thing. Everybody got enough to eat, even if there was little variety and few treats. But we were almost all thin (by today's standards) and healthy! If only we still had rationing, there wouldn't be this problem of obesity. But that's fantasy. We have to deal with the world as it is.

Throughout my childhood and early adulthood, the standard of living for most people in the UK rose steadily. So I never suffered the deprivations of my parents and grandparents. Good luck to me for being born at the right time. And I do mean the right time. I fear for the present generation, with all this junk food, fizzy drinks, lack of exercise, worries about paedophiles, rising crime, international terrorism and so forth. It's a sad fact, but it looks as though the next generation are going to be the first to die younger than their parents have. Incredible!

Well may those of us of my generation congratulate ourselves on reaching our sixties relatively unscathed. But there still remains the question of what we do with our lives for the remaining thirty or forty years which now appear to be allotted to us.

Thirty or forty years more

Yes, thirty or forty years more. Most of us alive today will reach our eighties, if we haven't already done so. Vast numbers of us will get into our nineties, and there'll be so many of us who reach the century that the Queen, or whoever is the monarch after her, will have a full-time job sending out congratulatory telegrams to us centenarians by the daily sack-load. But that doesn't explain why I've waited so long before starting this book. Well, I've been busy. In any case, when I passed the sixty mark I thought of myself as being "in my early sixties." I kept up that pretence at least until the age of sixty-four, by which time I could say that I was in my middle sixties. Then I thought, at what point do I move into my "late" sixties?

Since I gave up my business at the age of sixty-three to become a full-time writer, I have had this book in mind. By now I've had nearly three years' experience of being as it were footloose and fancy free with my time, thanks to the continuing financial support of my dear wife. Is it now the time to let the world of the elder person have the benefit of my experience? Perhaps a few under-sixties will read my words and take the appropriate action. As well as "do it now", I would say "plan ahead." So here are a few tips as to how you might spend your time for the next few decades. In this book there are literally thousands of suggestions. I am not saying that you should do them all – that would be impossible. Nor is there is one particular one line of action for you to follow. But hopefully there's something in this huge rag-bag of ideas that might spark you off to a more productive and satisfying last few decades of your life.

I don't want to be morbid, and indeed I am not at all morbid, but we all have to die sometime. The main thing is to make the most of the time we've got, however long or short that may be. Of course we could all go at anytime. Even the fittest and healthiest person can have some unknown internal weakness that could strike them down at anytime. And any of us could walk under a bus, if that were possible. But the fact that you may be called to your Maker at any moment does not excuse you from being inactive and wasting the time that you have got.

This book is mainly directed at men, blokes like me. Not that women won't learn something from reading it, as I'm sure they will do. But not being a woman, I can't pretend to understand what goes on in the feminine mind. What man can? But don't misunderstand me, I'm all for women doing everything that they want to do. I don't have any hang-ups about the fact that women can do any job as well as a man. It's a fact. Not only that, in many ways women are better then men. For example, in "multi-tasking" and "lateral thinking." This is in contrast to my own character and personality. I tend to be single-minded about what I am doing. When I see a task before me, I concentrate every ounce of effort and energy into doing that task and completing it successfully, setting everything else aside. Then, when that task is done, I turn my mind to the next task and concentrate on that. And so on. That's the way I am. No doubt there are many men who, like my good wife, are lateral thinkers and multi-taskers, but I'm not one of them.

My Dad was a brilliant writer. He wrote books, plays, radio, television and film scripts, and a stage musical. He was also a fine musician and song composer – but all in his spare time. Stan could and should have gone full-time as a writer, but he never did, despite often saying that he would. No, he stuck to his "day job" as an insurance agent. He was still working almost to the day he died, aged 81, but still in insurance. I had begged Dad to write his autobiography, but he never did. When his final decline had set in, I asked Stan to tape-record his memories. He didn't do that either.

My mother Helen wrote an excellent story of her early life which she called "*Empire Street*". It's a marvellous story of a young girl grew up in deep poverty in industrial Manchester in the 1920s and 1930s. Stan promised my mother he would "write it up" and get it published, but he never did. So I took on the task and the result was my first book, "*Nellie's Book*". And I gave up my "day job" – running my own press agency – to write full time. For all that I miss the day-to-day involvement in investigating and writing news and sports stories, and the adrenalin rush of constantly having to meet tight deadlines, I have never regretted it.

Now I'm at the age that my grandfather died, I have had to accept that you can't do everything. So you have to make a choice. In my case, I gave up one thing I loved (journalism) to do another (writing books) I love equally. I'm not suggesting for one moment that everyone should follow my example, but I am convinced that a change of lifestyle will bring you a fresh perspective, and help you live longer – and more happily. None of us know what's round the corner. It might be a heart attack, or walking under a bus, or whatever. If there's something you really want to do, don't let anything stand in your way, not even the day job. Begin it now.

Get the old Band together

I am fortunate to have been born at just the right time when rock and roll and puberty arrived together. I insist that me and my generation are the first and only genuine rock and rollers. We are happy that each succeeding wave of youngsters has enthusiastically taken up this new music, in its various forms. Popular music has never been the same since Elvis started to shake his hips. In my day, it was more or less compulsory for every teenage boy to belong to a rock or pop group. In my case I started with a skiffle group I moved on to various rock and roll bands, a folk-and-blues group, traditional jazz band, mainstream jazz and even a dance band. Playing for dancing was a great thing. It also enabled me to earn a little bit of money to help me through university.

So, why not get the old band together again? It's bound to be a great social occasion, reminiscing about what you did in your youth, even if you don't actually start playing again. But why not dust off the old instruments, or get new ones? It doesn't take too much to get back into the basics. Rock and roll was always easy to play, that's part of its charm. We were somewhat more than three-chord merchants, but the main thing is we had a lot of fun. And it might open the eyes of a younger generation to prove that grandad really was "with it" at one time. You could of course cause a great deal of hilarity by dressing up in your old costumes, drape jackets, drainpipe trousers, blue (or in my case, black) suede shoes, etc. I wouldn't necessarily advise you to go back on the road again. Just stick to small, family gatherings. I toyed with the idea of getting one of my old bands together for my sixtieth birthday, but it proved totally impractical. But I did get a band that was a contemporary of ours, and I'm happy to say they were as good as ever. Long live rock and roll!

Experiment

I've got to be careful here. I don't want you elderly blokes going off paragliding and breaking your necks, and me being blamed by your weeping widows. Nor do I want you grannies getting the rough end of some wild experiment-ation. But there's no reason why you shouldn't try some-thing new. On the contrary, there's everything to be said for it. If you really are happy, jogging along, doing the same old thing day in, day out, then good luck to you. But I will guarantee that most of us will get a thrill and perhaps a new lease of life by trying something different. Just keep your eyes and ears open for what is happening in the world around you.

Surf the Web. Read newspapers. Listen to the radio. Don't just leave the telly on as some sort of moving wallpaper. Surf the channels (or better still, check out the newspaper or tv magazine) and look for some different type of programme, something that will interest and excite the imagination. Instead of just saying, oh, I'd like to try that, get on and do it.

Risks within reason

This speaks for itself. I think it's a mistake to try and wrap kids in cotton wool. Every generation has to learn to take risks. Of course, we seek to protect our children from danger, but if children are never exposed to any form of danger whatsoever, they will simply never learn about life. All sport is dangerous, to a greater or lesser extent, but where would we be if sport were abolished? I rest my case. For the older generation, we need to use a bit of common sense because there is no-one to advise us what not to do.

But the same thing applies, as to children. You can't wrap us old folks in cotton wool, not if we are still to lead interesting lives.

If you are going to blow your savings on a trip round the world, leave something in the bank for you to come back home to. While I was running my own small business for thirty years, I knew that every day I was skating on thin ice. That was part of the thrill of it, never really knowing what was going to happen next or whether I would still be in business in a few weeks' time. More recently I have embarked on a new line of work, even less secure than journalism (if that's possible). But I would not and could not have done this without knowing that my wife was there to bail me out if I fell flat on my face. So I have taken risks, and still do so, but I do have a safety net.

Take risks by all means, but don't risk everything. You don't want to have gone through sixty years of life to build a reasonable lifestyle, only to throw it all away in your latter years. If you're single and no-one depends on you, then do it if you really want to. Otherwise, you will have just as much enjoyment taking a small to medium risk rather than the huge one.

Learn to swim (or surf or ride or fly or ski)

Why not? If I can venture out onto the skating rink for the very first time in my life at the age of 63, possessing no balancing powers whatsoever, I'm sure the least you can do is get into the water and learn how to swim. After all, the water supports your body. It also hides it. Beneath the surface, those bumps and bulges that you have somehow acquired over the years disappear from view. With a smile and a wave, you can be as handsome, glamorous or as athletic as you wish to appear to be. I'm all for swimming for all ages. As a journalist, over the years I have reported on a lot of swimming galas, and it always gave me a great kick to see youngsters competing. Little kids of eight or nine years of age, swimming their hearts out in the relay team, with their parents screaming themselves hoarse on the sidelines. It's fantastic for everyone concerned.

Swimming is a great sport and a great discipline for kids. The values they learn as youngsters will last them throughout their lives. There's the health benefit and the introduction to a sport they can enjoy for the rest of their lives. There's also the discipline of regular training, the benefit of improving their techniques and times, and the tremendous satisfaction of competing for a team. There is so much to be said for swimming, I honestly wish it was compulsory for every child from the year dot. And I do mean the year dot. I see little kids of no more than a few weeks old swimming happily with Mum and Dad – and Nana and Grandad. It's a great sight. You can learn to swim at any age, or take it up again. Swimming is like riding a bike – you never forget how to do it.

There's the sport, and the social side. Women and men equally can take to swimming as a good and healthy regular exercise. It doesn't take too long, and it can be fitted in at most times of the day. And you can swim for as long as you like. A touching tale: the highlight of a veterans' swimming competition was the sight of an eighty-year old man helping his one-hundred year old father into the water! Yes, you can compete up to the age of a hundred if you wish. There are plenty of people I know competing in their seventies and into their eighties. Quite a few people have discovered, on returning to swimming, that they are as good as if not better than when they used to be in their raw youth. This may seem amazing, but the fact is that some people returning to swimming at forty or even fifty have done lifetime best times. They find that with regular training, specialist coaching and dedicated application, they can get their times down to close to what they did in their teens and twenties when they didn't take it too seriously.

Don't just try swimming. There's nothing wrong with surfing. You don't have to be like those macho California boys and go standing up on your board from day one. You can get a lot of pleasure from body surfing and paddling about in the shallows. Try horse riding. Like everything else, it needs a bit of practice under supervision, but for many people it's a good way of getting exercise out in the open air. Then there's all kinds of flying, from hang-gliding to gliding to piloting a powered craft, from a microlight to a jet. It's all there. Just try it.

Beware the reborn Biker

Everyone knows the phenomena of the "born-again Biker", a middle aged man who takes up motorcycling after a gap of twenty, thirty or forty years. Sadly, many men have died getting back on their motorbikes after so many years. It's easy to understand why. We older men do not readily accept that when we get back onto a motorcycle, we need to relearn to some extent. Because we were dashing in our youth, we want to be dashing again. We may be fatter than we used to be, but we are very probably not fitter. Bikes nowadays are undoubtedly much more powerful than used to be the case, and the roads are far, far more dangerous. The reason that lots of middle-aged men are killed after buying a new motorbike and taking to the road years after giving it up is all too obvious. With a bit more money at his disposal, the temptation is to get something that bit bigger than he used to have - so much more macho. He hasn't had experience of being dependent on only two wheels for a couple of decades. By all means get back to motorcycling. It can be a great joy and a terrific social adventure. But for everyone's sake, take it in easy stages before you start burning the rubber on some 750cc monster.

It's hard for any bloke to admit that he's not as good as he used to be. But a little humiliation or humble pie can earn you a "lorra, lorra" years of life, and a much happier life. So why not accept yourself as you are, a middle-aged, reborn biker, who simply wants to relive the wild days of his youth? Start again by all means, but why not take up recreational biking, going out with the lads, as you used to? Some of those cafes are still there, some even still with their original juke-boxes. And bikers always have something to talk about. You might interest your teenage son or grandson in taking up biking. That will give you the opportunity to act as the wise old man and teach good manners on the road and safety on the road. For bikers there's a great thrill in traversing the open road, swift as the wind. I won't knock it, all though it's not for me. But if it is for you, be cautious, stay alive, and enjoy it to the full.

I'm not so much in favour of powered sports, for all I know that they mean a lot to many people, both participating and to watch. For me, powered sport doesn't require the same level of fitness as doing something under your own steam, so I mark it down on health grounds. But I'm all in favour of people taking up the hobbies and pastimes of their youth and thereby giving themselves a new lease of life.

Learn a language

Many people are frightened of trying to learn a foreign language. Don't be. Take lessons at your local college, or buy learn-at-home tapes. Next time you go abroad, try speaking the local lingo, even if it's only to order a coffee or to book a ticket on the bus or metro. It's great fun!

Age is no barrier

Many of our prime ministers have started the job at a comparatively late age. Most notably, Winston Churchill was 65 when he took over as PM in 1940 at our nation's lowest ebb before leading us to victory in WW2. After a second term, Churchill finally gave up the job at 77. Clement Atlee became prime minister at 62, Jim Callaghan at 64. Lord Palmerston first became PM aged 61 and was serving his second term when he died at 83. William Ewart Gladstone had four terms as PM, starting as a mere stripling of 59 before finally leaving office at 85. His rival Benjamin Disraeli was briefly PM at 63, but had to wait until he was 69 before having a second term which ended in 1880 when he was 75. David Lloyd George was PM 1916-1922 after introducing old age pensions as chancellor of the exchequer in the pre-war Liberal government. He was an MP for 65 years. It was only at the end of his career that he married his long-time mistress Frances Stephenson and was made an earl. Charles de Gaulle first became president of France at 67 and finally gave up the job eleven years later. Queen Elizabeth I reigned for forty-five years, relinquishing her grip on power only on her death aged seventy.

----------§----------

20

At sixty-four, former Beatle Sir Paul McCartney shows no sign of slowing down "When I'm Sixty-Four". He has put out a new album and live concert DVD [1]. Old rockers "Wayne Sheridan and the Wanderers" from North Tyneside re-formed themselves as "The Wrinkly Rockers" forty years after they originally split up, and are again performing at local clubs [2].

My musical hero, skiffle king Lonnie Donegan, refused to stop working despite a heart condition and died in 2002 aged 71 in the middle of his latest British tour. Glasgow-born Lonnie had three number one hit records in the rock and roll era. He is best known for "*Rock Island Line*", "*My old man's a dustman*" and "*Does your chewing-gum lose its flavour (on the bedpost overnight)?*"

The Queen and Prince Philip hosted a "Serving Beyond Sixty" lunchtime drinks reception at Buckingham Palace. Those attending included East Enders actress June Brown (79), Father of the House of Commons Alan Williams MP (75), actor Richard Briers (72), entertainer Bruce Forsyth (78), author Frederick Forsyth (67) and television presenters Sir David Frost and Sir Trevor McDonald (both 67) [3].

Chapter Two

"I'VE ALWAYS WANTED TO...."

Always have a goal in life

Be honest. No matter what your age, I'll bet there's at least one thing – and probably lots of things – that you think you'll do, one day. But supposing that day never comes? Virtually every man and woman on the planet has said to themselves on occasion, and often to their loved ones, "I always wanted to ...."

Ok, now's the time to do something about it. Because if you don't do it now, it's just not going to happen. If you want to be brutally honest with yourself and your family and finally admit that you've just been romancing all these years and in fact never meant a single word you said, then so be it. But that really is a way of losing face and losing faith in yourself. We all have to have a dream. And it may be better for that dream to remain a dream rather than have our hopes shattered on the rocks of cruel disappointment. But if your goal is genuinely reachable, then why not reach for it? It is important always to have something to look forward to.

This should be the longest section in this book. You should always have something on the horizon. If I was to have a gravestone, what I would like to have on it is "there's just one more thing I want to do." I think this is much better than Spike Milligan's "I told you I was ill".

I would have liked to have been a rock and roll star. As a

teenager in the 1950s, it was more or less compulsory for lads to be in a rock and roll band, and I was no exception. We did get as far as making a demo disc, and we did play for money quite a few times, but that's as far as it got - so I suppose our ambition was partly fulfilled. Then I wanted to be a champion athlete. That didn't happen either, but I've been in a lot of races and have had a lot of satisfaction and enjoyment from competing. Then I wanted to be Prime Minister....

Climb Everest, parachute jump

Obviously, as you get older, certain things are beyond your measure, and you have to accept that. I admire Brian Blessed, the ebullient actor. He was determined to climb Mount Everest and eventually did so, at sixty. It was a dangerous thing for him to do, but he did it and good on him. Lots of "old" people now are leaping out of aeroplanes and having their first parachute jump at a comparatively late stage in life. Nowadays, this is done by being strapped to a younger person who pulls all the strings etc. It's not something I really want to do (and my wife has absolutely banned this activity, along with bungee jumping and golf) but it seems pretty safe when done under qualified supervision. And you could always do it for charity, or to mark a particular birthday or anniversary etc. and your family will be thrilled (well, most of them will).

Visit lots of countries

Have you always wanted to visit certain countries? Well, now's your chance. Decide where you want to go, what you want to see, and how long you want to be there. And then find the cheapest and easiest way of travel, and go for it. Write lots of postcards and take lots of photographs. Both will stand you in good stead for the future when this trip of a lifetime is only a memory. If you're not quite so adventurous, you could always stay in your home country and visit lots of counties!

A few years ago I was fortunate to go on an official visit to China. It was fascinating to meet the Chinese people, almost all I met seeming to be hard-working and friendly. Even then it was apparent that this sleeping giant was set to become the world's greatest economic power before too long. More recently, I have been able to visit several European capitals of countries which have recently joined the EU. This has always been on business, but meeting people of different races and cultures, as well as seeing the local architecture and something of the countryside has been a life-enhancing experience for me.

With the growth of budget airlines, if you can choose your time of travel you can get some real bargains. And if you can surf the net, you can also find cheap places to stay. Remember, there is freedom of travel to all 27 countries in the EU, and it's easy to get to many other countries as well.

I like travelling, but not just for its own sake. I'm always happy to travel with a purpose. That's where family history comes in. It's a great excuse to go to different places and it gives you an objective, a purpose and a direction. And if you can so arrange matters so that the travelling is itself a pleasure, then so much the better. The holiday should start the minute you leave the house. And there's a lot in the saying "it is better to travel hopefully than to arrive".

Look up old schoolfriends

There are plenty of websites to help reunite you with your old friends and schoolmates. But again, be a little wary. Your natural pleasure and enthusiasm in greeting an old pal may overcome your better judgement. Old romances may be rekindled, and you could get burned. But I'm sure there's a big kick to be got out of "Friends Reunited". Seeing old friends or even relatives the first time in decades is not a sure-fire success, although I find it usually is. It's worth a try.

You might even like to get out a piece of paper and write down all the things you've never done that you would like to do. Cross out the impossible ones which you simply can not do due to your age and condition or financial circumstances, then look at the rest. Pick one or two and go for them. Then you might try something else. And so on. Always have something new on the horizon. This is not to say that you should interrupt your pattern of life, if maintaining a regular routine is conducive to your well-being.

Set yourself a target

Take some time out to think about the future. Imagine where you would like to be in five, ten or fifteen year's time. You might decide that you want to move house, either because you want to live elsewhere or because your present home does not suit you or will not suit you in future years. In other words, you might want to move to a smaller house, a bungalow or a flat, one with a smaller garden. You might decide to write your life story, or write a history of your local town or village or football or cricket club. You might get involved in a fund-raising effort for a local hospital charity or something for your local school. Having a goal, having an object in life, is something that everyone needs. The worst thing you can do is say "from now on, I'm just going to put my feet up". That's a death sentence. You can be sure that once the brain stops working, the body will follow soon.

....within reach

This is just common sense. There's no point whatsoever in setting out to try and do something that you know in your own mind is absolutely impossible for you as you are now. The whole idea of having goals is that you have at least a chance of achieving them. Why not a series of goals, steps along the way? If you set yourself a target, it's great to be able to reach it, so make it a reachable target.

When I became a "born-again runner" at the age of forty, at first I had no clear goal other than to try and get reasonably fit. One day I was at the mother-in-law's and going for a jog. Now mother-in-law – now sadly deceased - was a genuine Cockney, born and bred within the sound of Bow Bells. I'm a Northerner, through and through. She was a Londoner through and through and was most reluctant to go north of the river, let alone venture into the wilds of the North East of England where we were living. "Why are you doing all this running?" she demanded to know. I'm not quite sure why I replied as I did, but I somewhat rashly said that I was training for the London Marathon, the first one as it happens, in 1981, Mother-in-law gave me a rare smile, an approving smile (even rarer). "That's good," she said. That was enough for me. Not only was I now committed to running my first ever marathon, at the age of forty, for the first time I'd actually found something that the wife's mother approved of. So I was in, in a big way.

Not only did I run the first London Marathon, I went on to run another dozen full marathons in the next decade. I also ran the first Great North Run (half marathon) from Newcastle to South Shields and did every one from then up to 2005 when I decided to make number 25 my last GNR. In my case, running a marathon was not such a far-fetched idea. I had been a runner in my youth, and I had the physical and mental equipment to train properly for the event. Now I know it's all very nice to "aim for the stars, and you might hit the moon", but if you want to see improvements in later life, I would suggest that you set yourself a very reachable target for your first effort. When you've made that one, you can set a new target a little bit further on, and so forth. And when you've reached your limit, the wisdom of years will tell you when to stop.

Age is no bar

Cervantes wrote part one of his tale *"Don Quixote"* at only 58, but did not complete part two until ten years later. Goethe worked on *"Faust"* for most of his life. He began in 1775, published part one in 1808 and part two in 1832 when he was 82. Edmond Hoyle published his *"Short Treatise on Whist"* in 1742, aged 70. Swiss psychiatrist Carl Jung published *"The undiscovered self"* in 1957, aged 82.

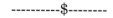

Stanley Kunitz became the USA's Poet Laureate at 95. He was still writing and publishing his poetry the year before he died aged 100 [1]. John Ducksbury, 81, from Richmond in North Yorkshire, has started a new business making non-alcoholic ginger wine. He is now planning to start another business selling pewter miniature models across Europe and the USA [2]. To qualify for the London Marathon, Peter Addis, 81, had to prove he could run the 26.2 miles in less than five hours, so he ran downhill. The Tyrol Speed Marathon starts near the top of the Brenner Pass in Austria, 1,219 metres above sea level, and is downhill all the way. Peter did it with less than a minute to spare [3]. Scott Baird made his Olympic debut at the age of 54 years and 282 days as a USA curler at the Winter Games in Turin [4].

After ninety years of gardening, 96-year old Frank Watson of Seaham in County Durham has produced what may be the world's biggest cabbage. The huge plant measures 16 feet in circumference and has more than 100 leaves, each measuring a foot in length and width. Mr. Watson, a retired miner, started gardening as a child and grew vegetables and kept hens and ducks to help feed his family. Recently widowed after 70 years of marriage, he has more than thirty (!) great-grandchildren [5]. At 83, County Durham pensioner George Hodgson has just done his first parachute jump and wing-walk. Thirty years earlier, he was told by doctors he had only a week to live after contracting non-Hodgkins lymphoma [6].

Pianist Ken Gray, from Consett in County Durham, is 100 years old and still plays the piano every day. Former steelworker Ken played in a Dixieland band in the 1920s [7]. Dr Anne Parkinson of Barrow-in-Furness, Cumbria, gained her PhD at 87 and is still researching at 90 [8]. Old Harrovian peer Lord Deramore had his first erotic novel published – after years of failed attempts - when he was 85. Richard Arthur de Yarburgh-Bateson, who became the 6th Earl of Deramore, was a wartime bomber pilot. In his youth he raced sports cars and set a cycling record of 149 miles in a day. He insists the erotic passages in his books are not autobiographical [9].

Chapter Three

TO WORK OR NOT TO WORK

Consider your options – the world's your oyster.

Why retire? My Dad never retired. I absolutely intend to be the same. I may work less, but I intend to carry on till I drop. That's for me, anyway. Many people look forward to retiring from their job, and why not? The thing to do, is to make sure you are fully occupied after retirement. Nothing could be worse than going full blast until you get the clock and speech of thanks, then "relaxing" at home, doing absolutely nothing. This is nothing less than a formula for an early grave. I am not knocking retirement, far from it. In a sense I have "retired" myself albeit by changing one job for another with fewer deadlines. But I have seen too many men deteriorate rapidly after retirement. Without a focus and a purpose in their lives, and missing the companionship and socialising of the workplace, they simply gave up on life, and died.

Plan ahead

If you are to give up paid work completely, the great thing to do is to plan your retirement in advance, if possible well in advance. Most people in their regular jobs and professional lives have to plan ahead, make out budgets and so forth. Surely it's possible for you to do the same for yourself in your personal life? Obviously you need to talk with your spouse or partner and probably your wider family as well. Think about your future income and how you are going to budget, but most of all think about what you are going to do. Many people say, after retirement, "I have less time now than I had before". Well, that sounds ok. Sounds as though you've got yourself involved in lots of activities, local organisations and so forth. If it comes naturally, then good on you. But for many of us, particularly men, the self-respect of doing a job and getting paid for it is something that we would dearly love to continue on in later years, perhaps on a part-time basis. Again, finances come into this, and you'll have to make sure that you are not going to lose out financially by taking on a part-time job.

Formal retirement could well give you an opportunity to try something else. In my case, it was giving up my second career as a journalist to take on a third career as an author and publisher. I could not have done that without my wife's support, and obviously you need to talk things over with your partner if you are fortunate to have one. But I cannot emphasise too strongly the excitement and thrill you feel on taking on a new challenge. We all have hidden abilities or strengths which we were not able to bring to the fore in our regular work. If you have worked in some big organisation most of your life and then retire, you could strike out on your own or join a small outfit. Instead of working in the field of business or manufacturing, you could try something more creative. There's absolutely nothing wrong with trying photography, painting and so on. You might become a tourist guide, or get involved in community or arts administration on a paid basis.

No set age to retire

The formal retirement age has almost been done away with. Recent legislation has made it virtually illegal to make people redundant solely because of their age. And I am very pleased that another piece of recent legislation (and I'm not a supporter of this Labour government, but credit where it's due) has included age discrimination in the "six strands" now to be covered by the single anti-discrimination body, the Commission for Equality & Human Rights. Heaven help the next person who suggests I'm "too old" to do something (unless it's my wife).

So don't be too jealous of people who retire at a relatively early age. Even if they have a decent pension, it might not be the best thing for them, especially if they give up work altogether. Some of my contemporaries retired in their fifties. I do feel sorry for them. Although most of the ones I know have a fairly decent retirement income, in some cases inflation-proofed (the lucky b......s!). Ok, you can enjoy travel, and why not? But I look for a bit more in life than merely to see the world, as pleasurable as this may be. Now it seems that the formal retirement age will event-ually be done away with altogether, and I heartily agree. One thing that is going out of the window, and rightly so, is the difference of the retirement age between men and women. It is absolutely ridiculous to say that women should retire at sixty and men at sixty-five, when women live so much longer than men.

Why do women live longer than men? There are lots of theories. My first thought is that nature knows that it is more important for women to survive than men, and there-fore nature gives females the wherewithal to withstand famine etc better than males. Think about it. In any primitive tribe or group of animals for that matter, if all the males were to die off bar one or two, the organisation would survive. If all the females were to die off, bar one or two, then the tribe or group would probably disappear altogether. I also think that a lot to do with it has been the question of men retiring from work and having no role in life thereafter. Women always have a role in life, even after a formal "retirement". Women are the supreme multi-taskers. From an early age, girls and women are expected to do lots of different things, and to regard this as their role in life. Men are basically restricted to one role and one role only, and that is to go to work and be the breadwinner. When the man stops working and stops being the bread-winner, he loses a lot of self respect, or he can do if he doesn't find some other satisfying and/or productive activity.

So the mental strain that this brings can contribute to a man's relatively early demise. It always seemed wrong to me that when women had a life expectancy of seventy-two, they retired at sixty and so had an average twelve years of retirement. But men, retiring at sixty-five, had an average life expectancy at that time of only sixty-eight. So a man had, on average, only three years of retirement! That's ridiculous. These figures are now completely out of the window. As I've pointed out, if you keep yourself relatively fit and healthy and occupied, there's no reason why you shouldn't live into your nineties and beyond and have a pretty active life in the meantime.

Get another job

So why not spend some of those years in some form of paid employment? Think about it. The great satisfaction of work is to be paid for it. When you are paid, it means someone values your contribution to society. And then there's the social side. Men like to club together, and one of the main places they do it is at work. Do find an alternative. The one thing you must get over is loss of status. If you have been a captain of industry, it must be galling to step down into a more lowly job. But, given the right mental approach that lowly job could be your salvation. Also, think of the benefits you can give to any organisation, large or small, in whatever capacity you are working. There is ample opportunity for part-time work. Just look. Try something new, but if you are not sure, then look for something relating to your past experience. If you have extensive business experience, why not become a business adviser? You could help get the next generation of entrepreneurs off the ground. The hardest thing in any business is getting it started. With your experience and advice, you could set somebody on the path to having a successful business, and earn yourself some money in the meantime. What could be better than that?

When you go to work, any kind of work, you have to smarten yourself up to a certain extent. You have to get there on time, stay the course, have the discipline of completing a task. In other words, you have to raise your game, every time you go out of the house. When you were working full-time, you didn't notice. But when you've had the experience of not having to get up in the morning, you notice the difference. All those things you didn't like about work, they were keeping you alive!

A new business?

There are plenty of examples of people who have run a successful business for most of their adult lives and then retired only to return to the world of work with a new business. That seems absolutely great to me, as long as it's "horses for courses". It may well be that you will operate on a smaller scale than you did before, and you might look for something less intense and competitive than the operation you ran in your prime. But you have the experience, you still have the brains, and you've probably got the cash. So as long as you know what you are doing, get on with it. But as with everything else, set practical targets and stick with your plan. If it doesn't work, accept it as another chapter, close it and move on. You may well wish to help a younger relative with what they are doing, or seek to fill a gap in the market.

On the night shift

This is the sort of job I would consider as suitable for an older person. Younger people with growing families and other commitments normally find it hard to be on a regular night shift. But when you're older and your time is your own, then why not? It could be quite an interesting thing to go on a training course with one of the major supermarkets. For all their electronic devices and centralised stock control and delivery systems, big stores still need managers. And more and more are opening on a twenty-four hour basis. So why not consider a night-time job? It will mean a change in your habits. And you will have to decide when you are going to sleep, in the morning or in the afternoon/early evening. But you won't be at work seven days a week. A normal thirty-seven hour week could mean four night shifts, ie four nights on and three nights off.

Part-time work

Unless it affects your benefits and or your pension, do it. I can't honestly pretend to get my head round the myriad web of benefits and taxes, what is allowed and what is not allowed. Lots of people have told me it's not worth doing a part-time job, because they lose benefit. So you will have to check it out yourself. The advantages of part-time work for us older folk are tremendous. For a start, we avoid the weekly grind of a full-time job, while at the same time enjoying the benefits of social interaction and the feeling that you are doing something useful. After all, if you do something and get paid for it, it must have value. There are the financial advantages, subject to the foregoing, but that's not the main reason. The government is now offering us sixty-five to seventy year olds some financial incentive for deferring our pensions, and that's an option I have taken. I'm all for deferring taking your pension, provided you've got the financial security and protection. You definitely need advice in this area.

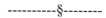

Workers who retire early are likely to die sooner than those who continue in their jobs [1]. The number of people working beyond the state retirement age could more than double within a decade because people cannot afford to retire [2]. Konrad Adenaur, West Germany's first post-war chancellor, first became Lord Mayor of Cologne in 1917. After being imprisoned by the Nazis, he led his country to democracy and economic recovery before retiring as chancellor in 1963 at the age of 86. German chancellor Count Otto von Bismark ended his 24-year term of office days short of his 75th birthday – a positively early retiree!

New EU rules banning ageism in the workplace came into force in November 2006. Advertising specifically for younger recruits will not be allowed, and firms will not be able to insist that job applicants must state their age [3]. John Elliott, founder and executive chairman of humidifier makers Ebac of Bishop Auckland in County Durham, said: "I flirted with the idea of retirement five years ago. Then I came to an agreement with myself when I was 60, that I would live another 40 years, but work another 20. Once you decide you are going to work for another 20 years, your perspective gets right again. You think longer term. Being 80 would not be a bad year to retire. Alan Greenspan was re-appointed as chairman of the Federal Reserve at that age." [4].

At 66, disc jockey Terry Wogan is still attracting big radio audiences for his breakfast show on Radio 2. Wogan is the most popular BBC radio broadcaster [5]. Nicholas Parsons (82) is back at the Edinburgh Festival Fringe for his seventh year as a chat-show host [6]. American political satirist Art Buchwald, whose columns were syndicated in more newspapers than any other writer, went on working until shortly before his death at the age of 81 [7]. At 74 Verdi wrote *Otello*; Wagner was close to 70 when he finished *Parsifal*; Bergman was 67 when he made Fanny and Alexander; and John Huston was 79 when he made his Oscar-winning film *Prizzi's Honor* [8]. DJ Sir Jimmy Saville presented the last *Top of the Pops* aged 79. He was the programme's first presenter in 1964 [9]. "King of the Blues" BB King finally gave up touring Europe at the age of 80 [10].

Ten per cent of pensioners are now continuing to work, and this will double in the next five years. A 91-year old works for DIY store B&Q, one of the first companies to actively recruit older workers [11]. Los Angeles bus maintenance worker Arthur Winston finally retired at the age of 100. In 90 years working he had only one day off, when his wife died [12]. Legendary folk singer Joan Baez, the "Queen of Woodstock", is still wowing audiences at the age of sixty-five [13]. Television newscaster Anna Ford presented her last tv bulletin at 62 [14].

New York's oldest barman was still working at 90. Hoy Wong has been serving drinks at the Algonquin Hotel for well over half a century. He counts Marilyn Monroe and Judy Garland among his clientele [15]. *"Tomorrow's World"* television presenter and WW2 Spitfire pilot Raymond Baxter kept working until the very last when he died aged 84 [16]. Edwina Bradley was still "going strong" at the age of 92 as PA to a hospital chief executive. By then, both of her children had retired [17]. Funny-man and supreme entertainer Ken Dodd was still going strong at 79. He had no thoughts of retirement [18]. Cardinal Cormac Murphy-O'Connor has been given permission to continue in post as head of the Roman Catholic Church in England and Wales a year and a half after the official retiring age of 75 [19]. Wild-life television presenter Johnny Kingdom, shows bags of verve and enthusiasm at 68. Veteran broadcaster Alistair Cook read his *"Letters from America"* on BBC radio every week for 58 years up to a month before his death at the age of 94.

Lloyd George's nephew WRP George was still working as a solicitor when he died in 2006 aged 94. He published his autobiography "88 not out" in 2001 [20]. Stage and film actor Griffith Jones continued working with the Royal Shakespeare Company from the age of 65, finally retiring at 90 [21]. Retired farmer Jim Webber, 104, is thought to be Britain's oldest worker. For the past twenty years he has been mowing, pruning, digging, weeding and trimming the garden of the New Inn pub at Stoke Newington, Dorset. Great-grandfather and widower Mr Webber works for a "self-imposed" wage of £3 an hour. He has never had a holiday in his life. He says: "As long as I'm able to do the job I think I should carry on to pass away the time." [22].

Sir Patrick Moore, approaching his 84th birthday, has the proud record of hosting his seminal astronomy programme

"The Sky at Night" on television for 50 years. It is the BBC's longest-running programme, and the world's longest-running show still with its original presenter [23].

Chapter Four

MONEY CHECK

Take time to study your finances. Make the most of what you've got.

We all know we should keep an eye on our assets on a regular basis. Reaching a certain age is a good reason to have a thorough review and overhaul of your financial position. First, what sort of pension or pension fund do you have? Insurances? Building Society and savings accounts? Tessas, Peps, Isas and so forth? Investments? Then there's your property. Even if you have no intention of moving, what about the value of your house? It's bound to be a lot more than what you paid for it, especially if you bought it many years ago.

When all comes to all, your assets are the tangible things of value that you will leave behind when you go (ie when you die). But for the present, with several decades of active life still left to you, now is the time to see whether you need to liquidise some of your assets and turn them into cash to spend on the things you want to buy. You might wish to switch your investments from one kind to another, or consolidate them in some way. If you are of pensionable age, you may decide not to take a pension or take a part pension and/or a lump sum, or to take your full pension entitlement. If possible, take independent advice. Your local bank or building society should be able to advise, but remember they are only allowed to promote their own financial products, so you won't necessarily get an impartial view.

Some people get very excited when they see the value of their house as possibly ten times or more what they paid for it. But this is an illusion. For a start, you can only realise the value of your house if you sell it. Then there's the question of buying another house, which obviously will cost you proportionately more or something of the equivalent of what you are already in. If you die, the value of your house will be counted as part of your estate and your children, or whoever you leave the house to, may have to pay inheritance tax. Then there's always the question of having to pay for your care when, if as happens to many people, you eventually have to move into a home for the elderly. The great thing about liquidising some of your assets in your sixties is that you can have money to hand while you "follow your dreams". The main thing is to take a sensible view of what you are worth and what income you can reasonably expect to have.

The other side of the balance sheet is of course how much disposable income/cash you will have available. By all means spend some "daft money" on yourself and your spouse or partner. Have a little fling, or even a big fling, but don't throw it all away. But there's no reason to scrimp and save in your old age, unless of course your circumstances force you to do so. Make sure that you will have a continuing income in your later years, and that your style of life will not exceed that. As Mr Micawber said in Charles Dickens' novel *David Copperfield*: "Annual income twenty pounds, annual expenditure nineteen nineteen six, result happiness. Annual income twenty pounds, annual expenditure twenty pounds ought and six, result misery." In other words, live within your means. But don't be afraid to spend some of your hard-earned savings on yourself, on little luxuries. After all, you've saved up for your "old age." Now's the time to loosen the strings, just a bit.

Avoiding Inheritance Tax

I'm not talking about anything illegal. Let's face it, the big, big bods with all the money can afford to pay expensive lawyers and accountants to make sure that they pay very little tax, and in some cases none at all. There's no reason why you shouldn't do something of the same, quite legitimately. I am not a lawyer and I'm certainly not a financial expert, but as I understand it gifts are free from inheritance tax if you hand over the cash or property seven years before you die. So as any of us may go at anytime, despite our hopeful expectations to the contrary, if you are settled in your mind that you want to hand over something to the next generation, then why not do that in the form of a gift? As always, do take professional advice. As with everything else it's better to do something about it sooner rather than later.

Book ahead

There are plenty of opportunities for cheap travel etc by booking at the very last minute. That's the great thing when you have time and the flexibility to choose when you want to travel. For lots of things, booking ahead is still the thing. You can choose the time of year and the route that suits you best, and make the most of what's available. Rail and coach companies offer these travel cards that give you so much off. If you are going to use them, and I see no reason why not, they may be well worth buying.

Time share, nightmare

The reasons why you are plagued on holiday in Spain and elsewhere by timeshare salespersons is that it is a very, very lucrative business. But for you, it could be a very, very expensive business indeed. You could so easily be landed with property that you can't sell. These salespersons beg and beg you to attend some sort of selling session, offering all kinds of incentives. Then you are subject to high-pressure salesmanship. Of course you shouldn't sign anything there and then. If this is such a wonderful investment today, it will still be wonderful tomorrow, and the week after. But I'm all for people enjoying themselves and making the most of their latter years.

Again, this is a subject to study in depth before making any moves. Time spent quietly in your local library reading up on the subject could be quite enjoyable in itself. Dreaming about having a permanent holiday home abroad, rather than actually buying one, might be just as satisfying – and at no risk! All I want to do is to caution against getting yourself into something that will not give you what you want.

So beware. I'm not knocking timeshare as such. I have friends who are perfectly happy with their timeshare arrangements. They have purchased so many weeks a year in such and such a place, and it suits them down to the ground. Fine. Time-share does suit some people, and provided you know what you are letting yourself in for, then it can be a fine thing. But make sure you really want to do it before you sign on the bottom line. The schemes to beware of are the ones where you are told you can sell on the facility, or flog off the weeks you don't want at a great profit. This is so often a myth. Sometimes you may be tempted by the ability to offer your timeshare to friends and family. If you expect your friends and relatives to use your apartment at certain times in order to defray the costs, talk to them seriously first before you make that big commitment. Check with them to see whether they really will take up your offer, otherwise you may find yourself with an empty apartment. And do look at the place first! It's amazing how many people invest, only to find that the apartment they have paid for is facing onto a blank wall, or a building site, or miles from the sea, or some such.

The same strictures apply, only more so, to these firms who offer holidays around the world on various schemes. All involve paying them money up front, and signing up for years on end. You can always sell your shares if you don't want to continue you are told. Oh yes? It can't always be true. No doubt there are good and bad in all these types of schemes, such as those whereby you buy points which can then be translated into holidays all around the world. If they work for you, fine. But I'm bound to be sceptical about having to put money upfront with the offer of cheap accommodation in exotic locations. I just wonder if this is as good as it is painted. In any case, all this applies only if you are a holiday person and want to spend a lot of your time travelling around the world, and have the wherewithal to pay for it. If you tick all these boxes, then great. I am not a holiday animal, so I suppose I am prejudiced against the whole idea.

Investment Clubs

Make investing a social activity. There may well be an Investment Club in your area. Generally they meet once or twice a month at some local venue where the members discuss the merits of various shares and other investments. Sometimes members will pool their resources for a particular opportunity to invest. Doing it jointly saves on dealing costs. The amounts are not large, and the club's success depends on the swings and roundabouts of the market. You don't have to risk any more than you want to, and most of all it's a great way of combining business with pleasure.

When to take your pension

This is something you have to think seriously about. I think the word "pensioner" is a misnomer. There ought to be a much better word to describe men and women of sixty-plus years. When life expectancy was much shorter than it is now, and everyone was expected to fully retire at sixty or sixty-five, then the word "pensioner" was apposite. Now it's definitely not the case. Even if you cease paid work after sixty or sixty-five, that is no reason why you should be regarded by society as "pensioned off". Just because you are not working for a salary, doesn't mean to say that you are not doing something useful. For example, carers, usually women, who are looking after children or their relatives. In general terms they don't get paid at all, but what they do is work as far as I'm concerned and it's just as valuable to society as having a paid job. Similarly, there's every reason why we should be regarded as being valued citizens of society, even though we are no longer in paid employment. I hope that everybody reading this book will either take some of the advice or, more likely, be already acting on it. That is, continuing to make a contribution to society, whether paid or not.

"Senior Citizen" – a proud title

The phrase "senior citizen" is not a bad one to use. As long as senior means experienced, wise and so forth, rather than doddery, old and useless. We are all citizens, and those of us in the senior bracket are going to be around a long, long time. And there's going to be more and more and more and more and more of us. Millions in fact. The time is coming when there will be more people aged sixty-plus than the rest of the population, so everybody had better get used to the idea. So society needs to look upon us senior citizens in a new light, and we should look at ourselves in a new light as well. Society must give us more respect, not only for the lifetime's work that we have already done, probably bringing up a family, and/or contributing to the economy, and usually putting in decades of hard work, but also for what we can do now and in the future – because most of us have a lot of future ahead of us!

Mankind has progressed by learning and accumulating knowledge, and by using that knowledge and experience to make things better for the future. Also, I like to think that senior citizens do care more about society in general, rather than their own personal situation. It's certainly the case that older people are more likely to vote in elections. Also, there is a great cult of the individual nowadays. Most people concentrate their efforts almost entirely on their own family, their own home, and so forth. But this is a very narrow view. If we don't look to the benefit of society in general, in addition to our own situation, then I feel we are missing a lot – as well as failing to help the general progress of society. The great thing about us senior citizens, who are hopefully reasonably well placed regarding our personal situation, is that we have the time, the knowledge and the inclination to do something for others as well as for ourselves.

Insulate the house

This costs very little, cuts condensation, makes the house warmer, reduces your fuel bills, helps the environment — just how many more reasons do you need?

----------§--------

In 2004 former Chelsea FC supreme Ken Bates put in £10m to take over as boss of struggling Leeds United at 73. Sadly for Leeds fans, they are still struggling. Veteran football writer Roy Webster was banned from going to watch matches at Wroxham FC near Norwich after reporting the club since 1976. But at 71 Roy has continued to write his reports, viewing games by standing on a ladder at the end of a friend's garden that adjoins the ground [1].

75-year old Lord Swraj Paul, chairman of the Capiro industrial group, is one of the richest men in India. He gets up at 5.45 am every morning and makes a cup of Typhoo tea. ("My nephew just bought the company, he's a very nice boy," he says). He then walks from his London flat to his office and does a full morning's work before going to the House of Lords in the afternoon [2].

To celebrate his 80th birthday, "Mr Smooth" — singer Tony Bennett — sang duets with Elton John, Bono and Paul McCartney [3].

Chapter Five

KEEPING FIT & HEALTHY

There's everything to be said for keeping fit for health and happiness – but why not make it enjoyable?

I would have liked to have called this section "getting fit" instead of "keeping fit". Let's face it, for most of us it's a question of getting back a little bit of the fitness that we used to have. The whole point about getting and keeping fit is not just to lose weight, although this is a benefit in itself. The fact of the matter is, if you are fit you enjoy life so much more. And you avoid disease. And you live longer. And you enjoy that longer life so much more. Everybody knows we ought to take exercise and keep fit. The trouble is, it's so often presented in the way of a duty, like paying income tax, rather than being looked on as being something to be enjoyed for its own sake. If you are going to get fit and keep fit, why not do it in the most enjoyable way possible?

I don't deny for one moment that some aspects of fitness can be tedious and off-putting. Jogging, or going to the gym, can certainly be tedious. And at times it can be difficult to limit your consumption of unhealthy food and alcohol. The way I look at it is this. When I see a chocolate biscuit, I ask myself which do I enjoy more, eating the chocolate biscuit, which will give me a few seconds enjoyment and a considerable amount of guilt, or keeping up my fitness regime? I like to think that in my case, the latter wins out. As long as it wins out most of the time,

then you are ok. To get and keep fit you must exercise. There is simply no other way of doing it. So look for the kind of exercise that suits you, that you can do within your own lifestyle, and which above all else you will keep up. That means avoiding boring routine and making your exercising as interesting as possible.

As for the food you eat, I can tell you from personal experience that it's just as enjoyable, if not more so, eating healthy food as opposed to unhealthy food. You may have to re-train you palate when you – as you must surely do – cut down on eating too much sugar, salt and fat. But when you've done that, the food tastes just as good. And you can enjoy the glow of satisfying self-improvement when you start to lose that excess weight.

Walk everywhere

You heard me. Walk everywhere. And I mean everywhere possible. Do you really have to take the car, just to go down to the shops, or to post a letter? The more exercise you do, the better, Walking is good. A reasonably lengthy (at least twenty minutes) vigorous walk every day will put you in good health and keep you there. Also, walking gets you out in the fresh air. You can walk anywhere and everywhere. You can see, hear and smell things you wouldn't imagine. Walking is perhaps the best form of exercise of all. In fact, walking made us what we are, the whole basis of homo sapiens. As I read my history, I understand that mankind's success came when we climbed down out of the trees and started to walk upright. Apparently, it was walking that gave early man the advantage over other animals. Once we had come down out of the trees and ventured into the savannah, we had a great advantage. Our ability to walk long distances and have our hands free meant that we could search for game and bring it back, and that we could move on from one place to another to find better conditions. Not only could we go a good distance to find prey, thanks to not walking on our arms, we were able to carry it home to the wife and bairns safely tucked away in the cave. Great idea! And then, when the grass looked greener on the other side of the hill (as it always does) man, woman and children could walk great distances. And so we spread all over the world.

So walking is a natural thing. Most of us can do it, so get to it. Whatever your age, try and walk every day. Man was built for walking. The one drawback is that, from the moment that mankind stood upright, we've had problems with our backs. However, I must confess that this is a case of do as I say not as I do. I do keep fit with running, etc, but I don't give myself time to go for a walk every day. But I do my bit for the environment by having a small car and not a gas-guzzler. And I do walk a fair amount, most days.

The stairs are your friends

Good slogan, isn't it? You get the idea. What I tend to do is to walk upstairs and get the lift down. My knees are not what they were, but they can still get me upstairs, thank goodness. Hope yours are the same. At one office where I am a regular visitor, they are so used to seeing me walk up the stairs that I daren't not do it, even when I'm in a hurry. Why not challenge your workmates to walk up the stairs instead of taking the lift, every time, and lead by example? Instead of "lunch is for wimps" (no it's not, it's essential to keep up your blood sugar etc) it could be "taking the lift is for wimps".

Find a friend

For many people, competition is not the thing. Walking, cycling, swimming and more dangerous sports such as skiing etc can be very pleasant social occasions as well as doing you good. If you can get someone to go with you two or three times a week, that is ideal. Just imagine, chatting to a friend as well as improving your health! Couldn't be better. The other essential ingredient of getting and keeping fit is what you eat. Forget the word diet, diet is simply what you eat. As far as I'm aware, for most people there is no magic diet that will get the pounds off and keep them off. If you found such a diet that suits you, well jolly good. For at least ninety percent of people, losing weight is inevitably followed by gaining it back. Eat less food that is bad for you and eat more things that are good for you. You don't have to cut out chips and chocolates altogether, but keep them within reason.

Cycling is good

About twenty years after becoming a new-born runner, I became a reborn cyclist. Running and particularly training for marathons was taking its toll on my knees, and I decided to take up cycling as a gentler form of exercise. As per usual, I needed competition to give me the incentive, so I entered some veterans' races. The first one I turned up at really opened my eyes. When I arrived at the venue, I honestly thought I had come to the wrong place. Standing around with their racing bikes were these dead fit blokes, slim, healthy, athletic, keen. Standing around and chatting, or seeing to their bikes, pumping up their tyres, or warming up on their static machines. I couldn't see one old bloke amongst them. I thought I'd come to the wrong event! Then I realised. They were all old blokes. But dressed in their Lycra gear, and with the enthusiasm of an event about to start, they all looked tremendous athletes. And so they were.

I've never really made an impact on the veteran cycling scene. For whatever reason I find it hard to get anywhere near the average lads, never mind the top men – and women. It has been a great enjoyment and privilege to have raced against the best old lads and lasses in the region. Like swimming, cycling is one of the best exercises around. You can do it in your own time, at your own pace, and for as long or as short as you wish. You can do it on your own, with a partner or in a group. It can be competitive, social or a holiday. You can do it all the year round, if you wish, or just when the weather suits. You can do it indoors if you wish. Now it's a fact there are lots and lots of exercise bikes lying unused in sheds and garages. Some of them have never been used at all. The fact is, it takes a hell of a lot of mental toughness to get yourself on the exercise bike and do enough hard work to do you some good, all on your own, on a regular basis. As with anything else, if that's your bag, fine. But I look at all those unused and abandoned exercise bikes, and I rest my case.

There is really nothing to compare cycling on the open road, with or without companions. Even if you are the most modest cyclist, you get a reasonable appreciation of speed over the road. You are out in the fresh air, enjoying the countryside. A word of warning: cycling is now a heck of a lot more dangerous than it used to be. It's not just a question of the roads being more crowded than they were in years gone by, the fact is that forty or fifty years ago, every motorist had also been a cyclist. Nowadays the majority of motorists have not been regular cyclists in their youth. Therefore they don't know how to treat us two-wheeled users of the roads. I'm not going to get into an argument about those terrible bikers who power along city pavements, scattering the pedestrians. I know there are such people. I do understand that in the city centre it can be highly lethal for a cyclist to actually try and venture along the roads. It is very tempting to use the pavements. All I am saying is there are some cyclists who spoil it by breaking the law in this way. The great majority of cyclists would be only too happy to cycle on the roads all the time, if only it was safe. At least there are more cycle paths being constructed – even if some of them are a bit silly.

I do feel a bit sorry for cyclists I see pedalling along with all their worldly goods hung about them on their back, on the crossbar and in their panniers etc. My ideal cycling holiday is to cycle from A to B unencumbered and have your luggage delivered by van to be there when you arrive. Now that's a real holiday. One day, when I've got the time, I'm sure I'll do it. If, like my wife, you don't like riding on the roads, then there are plenty of places where you can ride in perfect safety. Plenty of seaside resorts have now designated lots of promenade space for easy and safe cycling. Thanks to Dr Beeching, there are miles and miles of old railway tracks which have been converted for cyclists. And then, for the more adventurous, there are the long distance cycle tracks, like the C-to-C (sea to sea, coast to coast) route that links the east and west coasts across the North of England. That's another target for me. It always gives me a great kick to see a couple on a tandem, peddling away in harmony. Well, you can't really have it any other way, as the pedals go round at the same rate, you're bound to keep in step. You could always try a tricycle, or – for the more adventurous – mountain biking. And there's those brave souls who venture out onto the public roads on a recumbent bike!

The dangers of cycling on modern roads was brought home to me last year (2006) when I had a bad crash. I was competing in a triathlon and, after a good swim, I was having a good bike ride, bombing along a long, straight road on my lightweight, low-profile racing bike. A big wagon cut me up and, although I avoided a collision, I finished up lying unconscious on the tarmac after crashing to the ground. Fortunately, no bones were broken, but I was on painkillers for several weeks. Thinking about it afterwards, I could easily have been killed – my helmet saved me. But nothing is without risk. We can't wrap ourselves (or our children or grandchildren) in cotton wool, nor should we. Of course we should always take all necessary precautions, but if something's going to happen, it will happen. You can't avoid all risk, but let's be sensible and cut out unnecessary risk

Keeping fit need not be boring

There are obsessive people like myself who can go in the gym and pound away for hours, or run round the streets, or cycle long distances, and be perfectly happy doing it. But for most people, there is a much lower boredom threshold, which may be very, very low. But we need to exercise to keep fit and healthy. So how to overcome this problem? One thing is to have an incentive. If the incentive is powerful enough, it will help you get over the boredom of repetitive exercise, if that's the route you are taking. This came home to me at a very early age when I was in the Railway Club.

Now I'm sure it's still the case that you can buy lengths of railway track, already made up, and join them together in any way you wish. But we had one obsessive member of the club who insisted on constructing his own miniature railway completely from scratch, rivetting the track to the sleepers. This was all in Hornby double-O size I hasten to add, not full size. Now this guy spent hours and hours and hours rivetting, rivetting, rivetting. Repetitive, boring. Even I couldn't understand why he would do such a thing, so I asked him why. The answer was the satisfaction he got when he finished the job. That was sufficient incentive to carry him through.

For me, my incentive is competition. For all that I'm not a natural athlete, I love to compete. And if I can get myself reasonable fit and pick my events carefully, I can possibly figure in the top half dozen in my age group in a local event. That makes me feel great. And that's a good enough incentive to keep me going. At the same time, when I'm cycling, running or working out in the gym, my brain is free. I can write speeches and articles in my head, think about writing a new book, think of all the things that I would like to say to people if I was only completely free to do so, and so on. That does it for me. For most people, company is essential. That means joining a running or jogging club and going out with a group of like-minded people. It's a big encouragement, and it's also safer.

At my local athletics club, there is a club night at the running track which is our headquarters. I've noticed that, as well as the male and female competitive athletes doing their training, quite a few women of various ages turn up and simply walk round the track so many times. For them, this is a good way of exercising. They are in good company, in a protected and sheltered environment, with facilities to hand. For cycling there's a similar variety. My own cycling club operates time trials and cyclo-cross events for the competitive-minded, and there are also the Sunday runs for the social side. So it's pick and mix.

Swimming is another exercise that can be either solitary or social or both. Most swimming baths now "lane off" a section of the pool at certain times in order to give obsessive people like myself the chance to plough up and down and do so many lengths. For other people, it is a grand social occasion with some moderate exercise thrown in. It also makes sure you are very, very clean. Take the grandchildren to the baths – you'll have a great time. Or try one of the various exercise-in-the-water classes. Not only does the water give you support and provide stress-free resistance to help you get fit, it also keeps your wobbly bits out of sight under the water.

There are all kinds of variations of athletics, such as orienteering. You can arrange a cycling holiday whereby your gear is transported from A to B while you cycle along instead of having to hump it with you and so forth. I haven't even mentioned sailing, surfing and all kinds of other activities. The main thing is, make sure you exercise regularly. I would say at least three times a week. I guarantee you will feel the benefit. If you want company, I'm sure you can find it with a minimum of effort. As I've often heard people say "the hardest thing is, to get out of the house". In other words, once you've packed your sports bag and set off for the swimming baths or the gym, you are on your way.

The other advice I would give is to have as much variety as possible. I always vary my training, as I find it not only mentally helpful, but also on the physical side: you're not exercising the same muscles all the time. This is why I like the triathlon, as each part of the event (swimming, cycling, running) affects different muscle groups. And as stamina is my strong point, it's the ideal sport for me.

We were originally designed to run around on all fours, so standing upright does put a strain on the lower back. That's why I'm pretty regular at doing my "stretchers" every day. This is something which I'm sure is of major benefit. Lift your arms above your head, at least once a day, every day. This way you'll not only keep yourself as supple as possible, you will also avoid injury for when you suddenly make that movement or lift or grab something in an unusual way. What do animals do? If you watch any animal, a dog or a cat, the first thing they do when they rise from a recumbent posture is to stretch. And then they are off. It's like warming up a car engine, or at least with an old-fashioned car. I'm all for people taking vitamins. I am sold on the idea that tiny amounts of vitamins can do you good, so I try and cover all the bases.

Dancing for health and happiness

There's nothing wrong with dancing, at any age. In my youth, I was quite good at ballroom dancing. Not only did I take lessons, I was able to help my tutor with beginner's classes. Ballroom dancing is an excellent and healthy form of exercise, it involves the kind of music you probably like, it is a highly sociable activity: definitely strongly recommended for the social aspects. There are other forms of dancing of course, such as line-dancing, the more vigorous the better. Doing disco-dancing is a great exercise, the only snag being that it has to take place in a deafening cacophony of noise. But there are plenty of other things you can do that combine exercise and sociability.

There are all kinds of yoga classes, keep-fit classes and so on. You could learn to swim or indeed take advanced swimming lessons. You could fly kites. Or go water-skiing or surfing. All these things can be done at different levels of activity, and all under qualified supervision. The thing is, find something that is going to get you out of the house and mixing with other people. I'm a great believer in the strong connection between the brain and the body; stimulating one also stimulates the other. Try it.

What's wrong with a good argument?

Nothing at all, providing you don't lose your rag or get into a fist fight. There's absolutely nothing wrong with people disagreeing about any subject under the sun, including politics and religion. A really good discussion can stimulate the brain and make you feel a whole lot better in your mind. Obviously, us older ones tend to have fixed ideas about life, but that's not a problem as long as you take into account that other people also have their own fixed ideas. In fact, I do miss political debate and deplore the fact that we have so little of it. The place for debate now is down the pub or club. Now a debate fuelled by drink is not always the most sensible thing to have. People under the influence will make the most adamant statements which in more sober times they might avoid. But you can't have everything.

Exercise brain and body

One of the best ways to keep the brain occupied is to try something new, a night class or whatever. Although it's true, apparently, that our brains start to deteriorate even before we are born, that's no excuse not to use the bits that we have left still in working order in older age. There are a myriad of subjects to choose from at the day or evening classes at your local college. So go to it. Keep those brain cells busy!

This is for life

With both exercise and food, remember this is for life, not just for a few weeks before a wedding or your summer holidays. If you do regular moderate exercise and eat and drink sensibly most of the time, you will enjoy life more and live longer and more happily. Stopping smoking will benefit you, no matter how old you are.

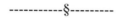

Dr Anne Parkinson of Barrow-in-Furness, Cumbria, gained her PhD in 2003 aged 87. Approaching ninety, she is still researching [1]. Don Karkos was partially blinded by shrapnel in 1942 but was still working as a "stable "boy" in 2006 at the age of 82 when a racehorse kicked him in the head and restored the sight in his right eye. There's a moral there somewhere [2]. *"Last of the Summer Wine"* television stars Peter Sallis and Frank Thornton ("Clegg" and "Truly"), both aged 84, ditched their body-doubles to get fit and now do a lot more walking when filming episodes. The late Bill Owen ("Compo" in the series) continued to work into his eighties despite, suffering from cancer. Comic actor Norman Wisdom, 90, made a guest appearance in the 33rd series of the show [3].

Iris Lindley's father taught her to dance the waltz at the age of four – and she has danced all her life until she had to give it up aged 94 because of a hip problem. Iris, now 100, said: "I never tired of dancing. It always meant the world to me. It kept me feeling really young and happy, and it's no doubt why I've lived to be a hundred." Iris and her late husband Alex danced together throughout their long and happy marriage [4]. Arts patron Margaret Gardiner took an early morning swim in Hampstead Heath pond throughout the winter. She lived to 100. But, beware.

Great-grandfather Michael Hammond, 69, died of a heart attack after taking part in a charity swim in the North Sea[5]. Hunter Davies, 68, blames his rheumatoid and osteoarthritis on playing football until he was fifty [6].

Bill Smith of North Cowton, still playing weekly five-a-side football at 80, says: "I still play up front. There's plenty of time to go into defence when you get older." Jack Watson, 83, is still scouting and has belatedly taken up bowls; veteran athlete Len "the Leap" Watson, has just turned 90; Arthur Puckrin, 65, Middlesbrough barrister and world "iron man" medal winner, is still running [7]. In his mid-eighties, the Duke of Edinburgh still competes fiercely in the highly physical and dangerous sport of carriage driving. He still has spills, and is deeply disappointed if he doesn't win. Prince Philip took up what he calls a "geriatric sport" at sixty [8].

85-year old Jim Purcell from Jarrow on Tyneside, is still running marathons after having two knee replacements [9]. 86-year old Harold Dodd of Wythenshaw, Manchester, still swims every day. He holds three British age group records from 200m to 1500m, and he won five medals, three golds, a silver and a bronze at the World Masters championships in 2004 [10]. Martina Navratilova finally retired from top-rank tennis at the age of 49, after winning her 59th major title [11]. 95-year old Greta Whitfield plays golf regularly, drives her car, plays bridge, hosts a Bible study class – and enjoys a glass of sherry [12].

Status, rather than wealth, prolongs life. Nobel Prize winners, successful war leaders, and senior civil servants all live longer than average. People who reach the top of their profession and gain success become satisfied they are at the top, and are therefore less stressed lower-ranked, lesser achieving people. Sir Winston Churchill, who won the Nobel prize for literature and led the country to victory in WW2, lived until 90. Philosopher and mathematician Bertrand Russell, who lived to 97, is another Nobel literature prize winner, as is Alexander Solzhenitsyn who is 88 and still with us at the time of writing. Oscar winners for acting and screenplay live on average four years longer than unsuccessful nominees [13].

Political reformer William Cobbett, who became MP for Oldham at 69, published his *"Advice for Young Men"* two years earlier. Cobbett was still writing and publishing his *"Weekly Political Register"* when he died in 1835 at the age of seventy-two. "Father of India" Mahatma Gandhi was arrested for civil disobedience in his seventies and was still a major political figure when he was assassinated aged 78. Ian Smith, former prime minister of Rhodesia, is still politically active at 84.

Chapter Six

PASTIMES & HOBBIES

Now's your chance to do something satisfying and fulfilling that you never had time for before. Something interesting that keeps those "little grey cells" working.

I recently joined a drama group for the over-fifties. Apart from the obvious fact of our appearance, in that we were all, well, a bit old, you could not tell the difference with any drama group that I've been associated with. Perhaps more daring, less inhibited. But all the usual jealousies, tensions and tantrums were there – but nothing to spoil the fun. Definitely recommended for loosening you up outside and inside.

Painting or even Art

Winston Churchill loved to paint. Although he was clearly a driven man and extremely productive throughout his life, he found painting a tremendous relaxation. But paint for yourself, not for others, unless you feel you have a particular calling. Painting covers a whole host of things. There's the type of paint that you want to use, whether you paint on canvas or paper or whatever, whether you do it indoors or outdoors, and whether it's abstract or representational and so forth. There are plenty of opportunities to exhibit your work, and joining a club or a painting class can give you a good deal of social interaction with other people. So there's something that can really occupy you and give you a lot of satisfaction. You can keep your paintings, destroy them or give them away to relatives and so on. The thing is, do it for its own sake - art for art's sake.

DIY skills

This is something that could and should apply to men and women equally. As a matter of fact, I am absolutely hopeless at DIY or any related subject. When you are retired or semi-retired, you've got a precious commodity – time. Plan it wisely. Just take on one job at a time, and don't find yourself going here and there doing jobs for all your sons/daughters, sons/daughters-in-law etc. Make sure that if you are improving someone else's house, that they pay the full whack regarding materials, even if they are a close relative and you give your time free. And if they do offer you something for your time, accept it. Something's better than nothing, they are saving a lot of cash by using you, so you might as well get something out of it for yourself.

One good thing about doing your own jobs is that you can put that bit of extra time in to give that real quality finish. I'm sure that gives a lot of satisfaction. If you are a bodger, recognise yourself for what you are and give it up. Sometimes it's best to be brutally honest, and accept, like me, you just don't have the touch. "Improvements to your own home" must of course be agreed in advance with your partner, if you are lucky enough to have one. Nothing could be worse than having a sort of "Changing Rooms" scenario in which your beloved one arrives back home only to admit gasps of horror as he or she sees what havoc you have wrought. It must be very dispiriting to have to do it all again because you didn't consult the dear one in the first place.

Remember, the whole point of DIY is to improve things, not make them worse. So putting up shelves must be for a purpose, eg for a specific collection of objects to go there, and hopefully to clear space elsewhere. After all, you are probably going to spend the rest of your life in your home, and that will be several decades, so you may as well make yourself comfortable and enjoy living at home.

If your house has some deficiency that constantly irritates you, why not do away with it and give yourself an easier life? You have the choice of how to arrange your surroundings, so go to it. If neither you nor your spouse or partner have DIY skills, and you don't have a handy relative who can stand in for you, then there's no option but to "get a man in". Or even a woman. Now there can be pitfalls here. You might be tempted to go to Joe Bloggs down the road, but if it's a "gubby job" you will have no comebacks if things goes wrong. Friendly Joe down the road might take your money and rip you off in some way, or do a bad job, or break off work only to return weeks or months later, or never.

I know there are many tales about professional builders, but you should be able to avoid most problems by what amounts to a pre-nuptial agreement. Write it into the contract that the job must be completed by a certain date. Specify all materials, and insist on a firm quote. You may have to wait for some time for this to happen, and you may find that a lot of builders shy away from being tied down. But I would rather wait and get a proper job done in an agreed time and within an agreed budget, rather than take chances. The one thing that will always bump up the price of a job is anything that's an alteration. So try and look ahead and avoid these pitfalls, if you possibly can. If extra work is needed, ask for a quote along the way. Check with your local council. They will have lists of approved contractors who have a good track record.

Dig for victory

What I'm talking about is taking on an allotment. Not everybody nowadays wants the trouble of keeping an allotment, so there could well be one or more going spare at your local allotment gardens. But don't take it on unless you can carry it through. It's likely that you'll be given an overgrown plot that hasn't been cultivated for two or three years. You'll have to put a lot of work in setting the garden, even if you use the services of a rotorvator for the initial work. You may consider taking on half a garden, which is still a quite substantial area. In any case, decide in advance what kind of crops you want to grow, whether vegetables, flowers or whatever. You'll find allotment holders are in general a very friendly lot, and you will get a lot of advice and some help. If you are a regular attender, and look after your garden, then you will be held in high esteem. What allotment holders don't like are people who neglect their gardens and allow them to become overgrown. This not only affects the appearance of the whole area, but it also allows weeds to spread to other gardens.

Part of the pleasure of having an allotment is to get away to a little bit of countryside, even in the middle of a big city. You'll find that a lot of gardeners have built their own "home from home" in the shape of a shed or whatever, with comfortable armchairs and so on. On some sets of gardens you will find a sort of headquarters building where the old gadgies will gather for a cup of tea, a smoke and a chat. Ok, they may be getting away from their wives, but at least the womenfolk know where they are and hopefully you will come to no harm in this milieu. There are also a good many excellent women allotment holders, I hasten to add. A big bonus is of course producing your own foodstuffs. There's nothing like home grown vegetables to give you real pleasure at the meal table. If you don't want to go any distance to tend an allotment, why not turn part of your garden over to produce?

We can all exercise

When I went to China I was impressed with the numbers of ordinary people who got up in the morning and went out into the park to do their Chinese-type exercises. In fact, I usually do a few stretchers myself when I get up. I'm not so sure about the peace and tranquillity of the mind, but if you can add that in, so much the better. I know that competitive sport is not for everybody, but I am sure that it is inbuilt in many of us. So if you can find a sport where you can compete on some sort of basis to give you the satisfaction of doing so, then get stuck into that sport. There's a big social dividend or bonus to be got from any kind of team activity. Being in a team means that you don't have to be a star performer to contribute to the success of the team.

Collecting

The great thing about collecting is that you can collect anything, absolutely anything. You know, you could be the only person in the world who is collecting that particular thing. A colleague challenged me to guess what he collected. Eventually I had to give up. He collects airline sick bags! Yes, this is true. But I bet there are lots of other people who collect even more abstruse items. So go to it. Start your collection. It may or may not be unique, and it may or may not earn you any money. But one thing's for sure – you'll have a lot of fun. Go to any collectors' fair, and your eyes will be opened – mine were. But there's nothing wrong with collecting stamps, cigarette cards, coins, autographs or any other form of memorabilia. Look on the internet – you'll find lots of ideas. And maybe some inexpensive items to get you started.

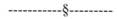

Daily mental exercises can give the elderly an extra fourteen years of alertness [1]. Surfing the net is the top pastime for the elderly, overtaking DIY and gardening as the favourite pastime for older people. "Silver surfers" spend an average if six hours a week online. Using the internet supports a less stressful approach to life [2].

Ellen Johnson of Berwick in Northumberland learned to read and write for the first time at the age of 77. She missed out on school through illness, and hid her secret until she moved into sheltered accommodation and was persuaded to join an adult literacy group by one of her care workers. "Though I found it difficult at first, I gradually picked it up," she said. An estimated 5.2 million adults in Britain have worse literary standards than those expected of 11-year olds [3].

Writer Ruth Sacks Caplin found success with her first screenplay *"Mrs Palfrey at the Claremont"*. Made into a film starring Dame Joan Plowright, it was tipped for an Oscar. Mrs Caplin, who lives in Maryland, is a sprightly 85-year old [4]. Sir Francis Chichester was 65, officially a pensioner, when he became the first man to sail solo round the world in 1966/67. This Devon man, knighted with Sir Francis Drake's sword, did not rest on his laurels. He died aged 71 after having to drop out of a transatlantic race. An advertisement seeking three pensioners willing to join a 50-day raft trip across the Atlantic attracted a host of applicants, including an 83-year old retired orthopaedic surgeon. The advert was placed by Alexander Spence of Aberdour, Fife, an enthusiastic sailor since boyhood. The raft, planned to float from the Canaries to the Bahamas, measures 45ft by 25ft [5].

Sir Robin Knox-Johnston became the first man to sail round the world single-handed and non-stop, aged 29. At 67 and by far the oldest competitor in the race, Sir Robin was again risking his life by taking part in the Velux 5 Oceans single-handed round-the-world yacht race [6]. Jazz Floats sixth annual Jazz Party at Sea planned to sail from New Orleans in December 2006 featuring "320 years of Jazz." The headline players were Joe Segal, Lou Donaldson, Jimmy Heath and Bud Shank, all turning 80 years of age [7]. Eight couples from the same ballroom dancing club have been married for a total of 417 years. Six of the couples, from Bampton, Devon, have been married for more than 50 years. The self-styled Golden Oldies all dance at the nearby Uplowman village hall [8].

Walter "Wally" Dalton, from Eastgate in County Durham, is still a passionate biker at 80. He regularly rides his Honda 650 Deauville on the roads, and has three off-road bikes: a Montessa 4RT, a Scorpa SY 250 and a 1961 Triumph 246 Cub. He still competes in trials riding, and still works part-time as a van driver [9]. Alex Henshaw, one of "the few" and now one of the very few surviving Spitfire pilots from WW2, took to the skies again at the age of 93 to mark the 70th anniversary of the first flight of R J Mitchell's iconic aircraft [10].

At 100 years of age, Laura Balfour does crosswords, knits, crochets and sews to keep herself active and alert. Still leading an independent life in her own home, Laura's speciality is sewing intricate tapestries [11].

Italian astronomer Galileo was still making discoveries in his seventies, despite deteriorating sight and hearing. He halted only when he became totally blind. French chemist Louise Pasteur founded his Institute in 1888, aged 66, and he was still working when he died at 73. Sculptor Sir Jacob Epstein, who died in 1959, was still creating new works well into his seventies. US architect Philip Johnson set up a new practice in 1992 at 86, attracting Donald Trump as one of his clients. Johnson died aged 98.

Chapter Seven

GET INVOLVED

Become a volunteer - a great way to enjoy life – make yourself useful and get satisfaction from helping others.

Your local Community Association is a great place to start. I've been involved in two particular community associations over a lot of years. The first one was based at our local comprehensive school. There were so many good spin-offs, I can't list them all, but the greatest satisfaction I got was seeing so many young people participating. This was a "joint use" scheme, whereby additional facilities were built at our local school, to be used both by the school and by the community at large. It was the first such scheme in County Durham, and it has been a great success. I believe at one time we had four hundred junior members. One good aspect of the scheme was the central coffee bar, where people of all ages could mix and mingle. I think of it as the heart of the place. The old folks had indoor bowls, then there were all the usual sports facilities, and the youngsters ran many of their own activities. There were all kinds of sections and I've no doubt there still are, so in short, there's something for everyone. Some people went for training and became qualified youth leaders and actually got paid for their involvement. There's nothing wrong with that. And I know that the people who staffed the office became a real part of the place and got enormous satisfaction from what they did.

Neighbourhood Crime Watch

It doesn't just have to be a community association, of course. Something else you can do to benefit yourself as well as the community is to join your local Neighbourhood Watch and link up with the various crime prevention schemes. I'm sure that these have had a big impact on local crime, particularly reducing casual crime. All you need to do is to look out for your own street. With a network of concerned citizens, you can understand how things can improve.

Be a School Governor

All over the country, schools are crying out for school governors, especially for small, local schools. There are reasons for this. Years ago, being a school governor was dead simple. You had very few responsibilities, and everything was taken care of by the local education authority. Now it's all different. Successive governments have decided to give more and more independence to all schools, and this has meant many more responsibilities for school governors. Governors' responsibilities now include setting a budget, the curriculum, performance-related pay, equal opportunities and so on and so forth. At the same time, schools have been affected by the general reduction in the number of people who are prepared to give up their time to be governors. But, having done the job for thirty years or more, I can assure you that it's enormously satisfying.

All school governors must have some connection with their local school or the local area. Some are appointed by the education authority, some by parents, some by the staff.

But then there are also the co-opted governors, who could be anyone with an interest in the school. You don't have to play a leading role, but any governor with experience of finance, business, sport or any other area of human endeavour, to say nothing of education, will be most welcome. If you contact your education authority, they will tell you which schools have vacancies. You could always write in on spec anyway. You don't have to be a school governor to get involved with your local school. Most schools will welcome an input from interested adults, but of course you have to make your approach in the right way. And any school nowadays has to make sure that its children are safe at all times. That means checking up on all adults involved with children, including staff, governors and any one else involved in the school. You may well have to be "checked out" in case you have a criminal record.

Youngsters are fascinated about the past and love to hear first-hand accounts. Now I was born in 1940 and so have very little recollection of the war, apart from those of a very small child. But I was asked in to explain what it was like living during and immediately after the war, with rationing and so forth. It was a tremendous session. Of course, the class teacher was there, and what I was doing was part of something that she was doing with the children. But the fact that I was able to speak from personal experience about what it was like growing up in the nineteen-forties and fifties, was a big bonus I'm sure. Many of us older folk have had interesting working lives, often working in industries that may have now all but disappeared. Mining for example, or working on steam trains or in the shipyards. Or you may have skills that are still relevant to youngsters today, and that includes all kinds of artwork, embroidery, sports and games.

One important job that I'm sure is needed in every junior school, is helping the kids with reading. I did this for a while, and found it enormously satisfying. Getting a youngster to read to an adult, with some gentle help and assistance, is a great boost to a youngster's self-confidence. I've found the kids coming on in leaps and bounds when they were reading regularly. Again, it has to be done under supervision, but think of the satisfaction of helping youngsters to advance in reading, which after all is totally fundamental to everything that they need to do in life.

I'm sure it's the case that when a youngster gets to be good at something or finds they are advancing in one subject, it has a knock-on effect on other things. One young relative of mine had problems when he moved into the "big school". Although he was an intelligent lad, he was always in trouble and not getting on very well with his studies. Then the games master put him in the rugby team and he had found his metier. A big strong lad, he was able to use his energies to good effect. The interesting thing was, his academic work immediately started to improve alongside his prowess on the rugby field. Eventually it was found that he had a musical talent, and that lad ended up as a music teacher. A great story, and one that I had nothing whatsoever to do with. But thanks to that games teacher, this lad found his feet in the world. Schools are always looking to raise money for the school fund, to take kids on trips and so forth. I've been involved in quite a few school trips.

Organisations

There are organisations for just about every possible form of activity, almost all run by volunteers. You could be one of those volunteers, and with the right set-up it can be very satisfying. As well as local activities, most organisations have national meetings. This is a good excuse to combine business with pleasure, to have a few days in a big city or by the seaside, in the company of people with the same interest as yourself. Find out when and where the meetings are, and just go along and introduce yourself. If you're not made welcome, look elsewhere.

Letters to the Editor

This is one dead sure way of getting your ideas published. Unless what you are writing about is seditious, libellous or obscene, just about anything is fair game for the letters column of your local newspaper. You can write about any subject under the sun. And you could get some very interesting responses. I am fascinated by the letters columns in various national newspapers. Clearly there are loads of intelligent and experienced people who apparently have nothing better to do than write about the most abstruse subject you care to name. There are whole strings of correspondence about apostrophes, hyphens, growing tomatoes, problems with computers and emails and so on and so forth. As I say, any subject is fair game. There's a lot of satisfaction to be had from composing a letter on some burning issue and then seeing it in print. A couple of tips: the shorter the letter, the more likely it is to be printed. And it's far better to make one or two points clearly and strongly then to obscure your text with dozens of different issues. So go to it!

Politics – always a role for you

Politics and religion: according to a popular but misguided concept, two subjects to be avoided at all costs. Now I can't speak for religion, although I have had some brief experience of it during a crucial period of my life. Religion is a matter of belief. So too is politics. Sadly, it is the determined view the great majority of British citizens that politics is peopled almost entirely by rogues and vagabonds who are simply in the business for their personal profit and delight. This is a grotesquely exaggerated view of the situation, and I suspect there is just a touch of guilty conscience about those people who condemn all politicians as being venal and corrupt. Politics is not some sort of separate world that is completely divorced from reality, as much as people might like to think it is. Politics is simply the way in which we organise ourselves as a society. Decisions made by politicians at local, national and international level affect every aspect of our lives and our futures. It ought to be worth more than a simple dismissal. It can in fact be an absorbing and worthwhile part of our lives, if we wish to participate.

Like all voluntary organisations, political parties are crying out for members. It's so easy to join. You can sign up through a website, by telephone or letter, or simply by turning up at a branch meeting. I can virtually guarantee you will be welcomed with open arms. But a word of warning: the danger is, you will be sucked in and given too much to do too soon. Resist the temptation to take on a position straightaway, if you can. If you simply want to be a helper or a leafletter, then say so. There will be plenty of time for other things. Taking part in local and national political meetings can be most enjoyable. You will meet lots of people, many with similar views to yourself. Hopefully, this will expand your horizons. You can get involved in debates, and at least have an influence in national policy (although this is a reducing benefit in all political parties nowadays). As a party member, you will get the chance to vote for candidates to be MP, MEP or even on occasion, your party leader and potential prime minister. And do go to your party conferences, regional and national. With so many fringe meetings, there's bound to be something to interest and in which you can take part, even if you never speak from the podium at the main conference sessions.

Single Issue campaigns

While fewer and fewer people are now getting themselves involved in political parties (something I personally regret), more and more people are getting involved in "single issue" campaigns. This can be to save the whale, to save the countryside, to ban or not to ban fox-hunting, to support or oppose particular planning applications and so on and so on. I do very much welcome citizens getting involved – that's the lifeblood of any democracy. So, if you feel strongly about any particular issue, local or national, then do get involved. Join the campaign, or if there isn't a campaign, start one yourself. With mobile phones, e-mail and the internet, it's easy to get the ball rolling. Start a petition. You'll be pleasantly surprised at the support you can get. And you could influence the outcome of that particular issue.

"You call that a knife?" 80-year old Winifred Whelan emulated Australian actor Paul Hogan in the film *"Crocodile Dundee"* when she confronted a hooded burglar in her home. The intruder was holding a knife and demanding money, but Winifred grabbed a 14-inch carving knife from the kitchen and shouted "that's not a knife, this is a knife." Winifred had to be restrained by her husband John, 82, as the two would-be robbers fled. They were subsequently caught and jailed [1]. Jack Chase was 24 when he was first elected to Caister-on-Sea Parish Council, neat Great Yarmouth, Norfolk. Apart from the war years, he continued to serve and was still a member in 2006 at the age of 100 [2]. Carmel Connolly, one of the British Legion's Poppy Appeal longest serving poppy sellers, was still running a stall at 95 [3].

Teddy Kollek was mayor of Jerusalem for 28 years until 1993 when, at the age of 82, he was defeated by Ehud Olmert, later to become Israeli prime minister. Kollek died in January 2007, aged 95 [4]. At 82, John Kirkpatrick of Carlisle is the oldest person to be served with an ASBO (anti-social behaviour order). He claimed he turned his tv up to top volume only to drown out the singing of his neighbour Tommy Dunn, 65, in the adjoining retirement bungalow [5]. A 70-year old former soldier with the Household Cavalry fought off an attacker and held him down for ten minutes. Neville Paddy was hit on the throat but managed to overcome his 34-year old assailant and detain him with a wrist lock until police arrived [6].

Still singing at 96 – that's veteran vocalist Nesta Chapple from Blyth, Northumberland, after an incredible eighty years of public performances in local operatic shows and church choirs [7]. Frank Flintoff is still active in his local Young Farmers' Club – at the age of 89. He was the first secretary of Helmsley Young Farmers in North Yorkshire when the club was started in 1932, and he's still going strong [8].

Firebrand Blackburn MP Barbara Castle, minister of transport in Harold Wilson's Labour government in the

1960s, later became an MEP and was still wowing party conferences well into her eighties. Dr Benjamin Spock, American child care expert, wrote his *"Common Sense Book of Baby and Child Care"* in 1946. Over twenty years later, at the age of 65, Dr Spock was in court fighting the US government's conscription laws.

Chapter Eight

FAMILIES!

Families – we have them, whether we like it or not. But our flesh and blood should be a joy, not a burden.

The message is, keep in touch! Relatives don't have to meet frequently to care about one another. If you have close relatives living in Australia that you can only see once every so many years, you still care about them and communicate with them. They all have their own lives to lead, as we have ours. But as long as we keep in touch and see each other occasionally, that's good enough for all concerned. You can gain from checking out your relatives. Communicating is easy. As well as the mail, there's the telephone, e-mail, the internet, audio and video tapes.

The Christmas Letter

More and more people keep in touch through the Christmas Letter. Despite some criticism, I feel that this is a good idea. Families tend to be scattered, and any communication is better than none at all. But do read the Christmas letters you get from other people. After all, you expect them to read yours!

Make a Wall Chart

Keep it near the telephone so that when your second cousin rings up, you can "remember" not only the names of his wife and children, but also little facts about them, what universities they are going to and so forth. Or you could keep this sort of information in a little notebook. Sadly, in this respect I don't follow my own advice, but I know I ought to.

Birthdays are important

Yes, they are! Put them in your diary, include all your grandchildren, nephews and nieces etc. It's the thought that counts, so don't be afraid to send cheaper cards. Greetings cards nowadays can be so expensive, especially if you want to keep up with all the birthdays and anniversaries.

Family History

Checking out your ancestors is great. It's quite easy at least to make a start, it'll give you a great deal enjoyment and satisfaction. It's a fascinating thing to do. Why bother with family history? I say, it's worthwhile in its own right. With the internet and the user-friendly Family History Centre in London, anyone can do it. Family history also give you great excuse to go to other places, going into graveyards, looking at parish records and taking advantage of the many excellent Family History Societies up and down the land. Showing members of the younger generation copies of birth certificates, photographs etc can usually interest them and make them understand that they are part of a much wider family rather than just the nuclear family that society emphasises so much nowadays.

Of course the family unit, ie parents and their children, is a major building block of society and is the single most important thing to most of us, but the rest of your extended family is important too. Your life can be so much richer if you can take in other branches of the family. The sooner you can pass this message on to the next generation, the better. Put your memories of the names of great-grandparents, great-aunts and great-uncles down in writing for the next generation. Writes names, places, and if possible dates on the backs of old photos while your memory holds out.

Bury the hatchet

This can be difficult, but the main thing is don't bear grudges. Bearing a grudge may feel very justifiable and it may give you some sort of grim satisfaction. But your dislike and hatred of someone does not affect them, however it certainly does affect you. I would say either ignore your enemy altogether, or be polite. Politeness costs nothing, it makes you feel better and it could produce beneficial results.

Wise Old Man

When I was a young man, I used to think that one day I'd meet a wise old man with a big white beard who would tell me anything and everything I needed to do to sort out all my problems. I had the kind of lifestyle when my emotional, working and political lives were often in such a tangle I felt that only someone with vast experience of used wisdom could look at it and make sense of it. This wise old man, probably with a beard, very likely white-haired, would sit me down and tell me exactly where I was going wrong and what I would have to do to put things right.

It was quite late in life when I finally realised that this wise old man did not exist and would never exist. I would have to sort things out for myself. Now I am not claiming in any way that my life is pure and simple now. I'm still in a tangle much of the time, but the difference is that now I don't worry about it. If I have a seemingly intractable problem, I sleep on it, and nine times out of ten things look so much better in the morning. And if you meet an immovable object, you simply find a way round it. You have to. Life will take you around it anyway, whatever you do. But I'm sure there are lots of young people in every generation who can, in their heart of hearts, delight in talking to an older person about their problems. But I'm not suggesting that you should set yourself up as some wise old guru who can instantly solved the problems of the younger generation.

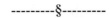

This year (2007) Sylvester Stallone is starring in "Rocky Balboa", the sixth "Rocky" film, at sixty. Veteran television entertainer Des O'Connor took over as presenter of long-running tv show Countdown aged 75. New-Yorker William Diehl, journalist, editor and photographer, turned novelist in the latter half of his life. He reached his peak at 70 with the publication of "Primal Fear", later made into a film starring Richard Gere [1]. At 84, Lucien Freud is still one of Britain's foremost painters. Recent subjects include the Queen, playwright Harold Pinter and model Kate Moss [2].

Chapter Nine

LOVE, ROMANCE - AND SHOPPING!

What is life without passion? There's still plenty to be had for all ages, and I mean all! Age is no bar to enthusiasm.

It's a sad fact that more and more people are divorcing in their later years. Our parents' generation often stayed together come what may, first for the sake of the kids, and then because of habit and social pressures. All that is gone now, and when people find that they are no longer compatible, they tend to take the practical course and part. In addition, there is a sad loss of a loved partner through death. Mainly it is the men who die first, but for many reasons the number of single older men is increasing along with the already large numbers of single older women. If you're happy on your own, especially if you have family close by or in regular contact, then you may well find you are better off as you are.

I've also seen cases where older men and women decided to marry but it hasn't worked out. Sometimes it's been after a very short courtship. When you've had a close companion for all of your adult life, and then you lose that person, it can be a very compelling thought to find someone else to fill the gap. If you were a couple of starry-eyed teenagers who wanted to get married after just a few weeks acquaintance, what would you say to them? Wait. Now you might say, oh, I'm older now, I can't afford to wait. But with a bit of luck, you will have many more years to live. Surely that's worth a few months?

If you are single and you meet someone else and you are attracted to one another, why not live in sin? Go for it. Marry in haste, repent at leisure applies to all ages. I could caution you, before taking the plunge, to have some sort of "premarital agreement" as regards to sex. It's all very well for young people to hop into bed at a moment's notice, as both can reasonable be expected to perform at the drop of a hat. Sadly, this does not necessarily apply to any of us in older age, particularly the blokes. Remember, the lady of your choice may well be expecting pretty high standards of performance in the bedroom department. If you feel you are not quite up to it, then the best thing to do is to be honest with her from the start. There's always Viagra!

Second (third or fourth) honeymoon?

Why not? It doesn't have to be with a different partner each time. It could be the same partner every time

Traps for the unwary older male (and female)

Remember, at an older age, we come to any new relationship with a lot of baggage. We can't help it. We've lived a long time, and we carry our past with us whether we like it or not. I'm not saying that this will necessarily prevent you from creating something new, but it could. On the other hand, don't deny yourself the opportunity for happiness if it's there, through feelings of guilt for a former partner who is now dead. The way to look at it is that this is a new chapter of your life. It doesn't invalidate in anyway the old chapters. You are not in any way being disloyal to your former partner. But just make sure that there is enough there to forge new bonds and be sure that you would like to spend the rest of your life with this other person.

Shopping for the older man

This is just for the men. Whether you have to go shopping with your partner, on behalf of your partner, or because you're on your own, shopping is a fact of life for most men of a certain age. But there is one way that we older blokes can over come this problem of shopping. And that is to take over the whole dam shooting match ourselves, at least, for food. When a man goes to the supermarket to do the weekly food shop, he is a triumph of a military campaigner. Not just a general, a veritable field marshal. A man sees a huge supermarket, with all its aisles and rows of various goods, as a battlefield. And when a man has a battlefield before him, he has a plan of campaign. First there is the selection of the correct receptacle for the foodstuffs to be purchased. This is a crucial matter. The advantage of the hand basket is of course speed and manoeuvrability, a special checkout for ten items of less – always keeping a beady eye on any fellow shopper with eleven or more items – and the knowledgeable campaigner avoids having to recover his pound coin, thereby shaving a few seconds off the campaign time. Because the number one objective for the male shopper is to get the whole job done and dusted and get round this maze of shopping in the shortest possible time.

The disadvantage of the hand basket, apart from trying to yank up the last one in the pile which is welded to its holder, the man having failed to notice the sign that says "do not take this basket", and apart from the restriction on the number of items to be bought, is of course the weight. More than one "blob" of milk, and you'll be suffering from an aching arm. That leaves the choice of trolley between a shallow or deep draft. A piece of advice: do not take the deep draft trolley unless you really, really need it. The shallow draft is much superior in that it is easier to place the goods in the trolley without damage. Transferring them to the checkout and placing the bags of shopping back in the trolley is a much quicker, safer and easier manoeuvre. Reaching down into the deep draft trolley to pick up a heavy item can cause back pain, if not spasms. But, of course, if your shop is a massive shop or a Christmas shop, then it must be the big bertha of trolleys. It can pay to test your trolley before taking it out, but that takes time. But if you find that your trolley if severely deficient in its directorial arrangements then abandon it and get another. There's nothing worse than being shown up as a man who cannot control his own trolley. After all, we men all think of ourselves as Formula One drivers. Pushing a wonky trolley shows that we are no such thing.

After a few expeditions to your local supermarket, you'll know exactly where everything you require is placed. You can then plan the shortest possible route around the shop. For example, you'll know which aisles to travel down for full or part distance, and whether to reverse direction in the middle of the aisle in order to get something at the near end of the next aisle, and so forth. It's known as "critical path analysis". Very few women know this. As with going to computer class, there is the added advantage of meeting people, especially your friends. If a man meets a male friend in the course of shopping, and they stop to chat, this is perfectly allowed within the rules. The time that men spend chatting is deducted from the overall time to go round the shop. The reverse, is the case for women, as any man will point out. The point about a man taking over the regular food shop is that no females need to be involved whatsoever. If you have a wife, a female partner, mother or daughter who insists on accompanying you, all you have to do is to suggest that they (a) go to another shop (b) find a place in the café where you will join her later, (c) attend the hairdressers etc etc. I have yet to see any woman allow a man to "take her round" the supermarket. It just doesn't happen.

Men who do their shopping on their own are looked upon as brave and courageous and are highly recommended. It means you can take part in conversations with female persons as to the relative prices of various foodstuffs, what bargains are on offer at any time and so forth. In some respects, it makes you an honorary woman, which at certain times is no bad thing to be. For me, I am a sucker for the BOGOF ("buy one get one free") syndrome. I just can't resist it. Now for example, we eat very little marmalade, as much as we both like it, it is very rarely on the menu. But when I see two jars of marmalade for the price of one, I cannot resist getting them. Result, storage space taken up with several jars of marmalade.

In other words, by taking over the food shopping, you have made a virtue out of necessity. You will feel so much better for it, you will be able to pick up the odd little luxury for yourself, you can buy those little surprise presents for the wife that women's magazines say you should to keep romance alive, and so on. You also need not concern yourself about the size of the bill. Indeed, you can congratulate yourself on keeping costs down, of course deducting those little luxuries earlier referred to.

That still leaves the problem of being dragged round Marks and Spencer or British Home Stores etc for items of clothing that your spouse or partner says you must have. Sadly, I have no answer to this. It is simply something that has to be endured. It goes with the territory. The only thing you can do, is to keep it to a minimum, and to extract some concession from your beloved one in return, such as an extra night down the pub watching the football.

-----------§---------

"Make time for a little romance every day" is the advice given by Britain's currently longest-married couple, Frank and Anita Milford, from Plymouth. Frank, 99, and Anita, 98, have been married for 79 years. They met at a YMCA dance in 1926 and were married at Torpoint Register Office two years later. It took Frank months to save up enough to buy Anita's £6 diamond engagement ring – he was earning £2.35 a week at the time. The devoted couple go to bingo twice a week and have regular visits from their two children, aged 77 and 72, five grandchildren and seven great-grandchildren [1].

Artie Shaw, clarinet player and bandleader best known for his 1938 recording of "*Begin the Beguine*", has died in Los Angeles at the age of 94. Shaw was married eight times, his wives including film actress Ava Gardner [2]. At 76, Sir Stirling Moss OBE suffered impotence (for the second time in his life) after having an operation for prostate cancer. He used the drug Levitra to resume his active sex life with his third wife Susie, perhaps aided by the fact that at 52 she is somewhat younger than he is. Moss headed an advertising campaign called "SortED in 10" – ED being Erectile Disfunction. It's a condition that affects 50 per cent of men over 50. "If you were having trouble passing water, you would go straight to the doctor," says Moss, "why not do just the same with erectile problems?" [3].

More and more elderly and middle-aged men are picking up sexually transmitted diseases, including men in their 70s and 80s. This is due to increasing numbers of older people finding themselves single. "Safe sex is the best sex" is the message for all generations, even if contraception is no longer an issue [4]. American entrepreneur Horace Hagedorn, who made "Miracle-Gro" the best-known plant food in the world, found his second wife Amy through a lonely hearts column when he was seventy. His first wife Peggy thought up the name Miracle-Gro. After Peggy died, Horace spotted this lonely hearts advert: "Winter weather causes this 48-year old, dark-haired, athletic women to read seed catalogues, listen to reggae, dream of sailing and yearn for romance. Where is the kind-hearted man with a cool head and a gracious manner who will share all my seasons?" Horace Hagedorn was that man. He and Amy (for it was she) were married for 19 years until he died in 2005 aged 89 [5].

An 88-year old farmer has finally fathered a son after 60 years of trying. Virmaram Jat, who lives in a remote village in India, failed to have children with his first two wives, but already has a 16-year old daughter from a third marriage. "I am a farmer with simple needs. I drink fresh camel's milk and I have intercourse daily. The best time is between 2am and 4am [6]. Pensioners have been urged to practice safe sex. People aged 80 are checking into clinics to have sexually transmitted diseases treated, according to Health Protection Scotland. Sexual consultant Ruth Holmes said "people are more frequently having relationships at older ages, with more partners and more sexual experimentation. You hear about swingers and you also hear about women going to foreign countries to pick up men. This would not have happened a few years ago." [7].

A 104-year old Mayalan woman wed a 33-year old man, her 21st marriage. "I hope this marriage will last," said Wook Kundor on tying the knot with her lodger, Muhammad Noor Che Nusa [8]. Writer Bill Bryson was asked what he would like people to say about him in a hundred years' time. "And the amazing thing is, he's still sexually active!" was his reply [9]. Arthur Jones, 80, was "on cloud nine" after being reunited with his wartime sweetheart after 62 years10]. Playboy magnate Hugh Hefner is still going strong at the age of 80.

A bride and groom were stopped by police after having sex as they drove away from their wedding ceremony. A traffic patrol stopped the Fiat Punto in Bergamo, northern Italy, when they spotted it veering from side to side going down a busy road. Inside, they found the bride sitting astride the partially-naked groom as he drove. The groom was 70 years old, the bride 59 [11]. The Rolling Stones, average age 62, were forced to remove sexually explicit lyrics from some of their songs while playing in the USA [12].

Former flamboyant parliamentarian Leo Abse, whose first marriage lasted 40 years, re-married at 89 to 39-year old Ania Czepulkowska. Abse has a son, 50, and a daughter of 48 [13]. Novelist Doris Lessing still has the power to shock at 87. The explicit language of her latest novel so offended a female proof-reader that she refused to continue working on it [14]. Dean Wooten, 65, store greeter at Wal-Mart in Muscatine, Iowa, was sacked after displaying a semi-naked picture of himself to customers [15].

The Seniorenmarkt (senior citizens' market) in Grossraschen, Germany, caters for the over-fifties and is looking to expand across the country. Pensioners have a bigger disposable income than any other consumer group in Germany. Retailers are taking "Best-Agers", "Happy-Enders", "New-Olds" and "Generation 55-plus" ever more seriously [16]. Writer and teacher Sybil Marshall published her first novel at the age of eighty. She turned to writing novels after being dropped by Granada Television as a contributor to their schools programme "Picture Box" at 75, after 23 years. At 48, she became a mature student and completed a three-year degree course at Cambridge University in two years. At 82, she married a man who left his wife for her [17].

Jack Archer went to buy sherry at his local supermarket. When he got to the check-out, he was challenged by the young woman on the till to prove that he was over eighteen years of age. Jack is 87 [18]. "Wrinkly sex": 67-year old Jane Juska created a stir in 2001 with her memoir "*A Round-Heeled Woman*" and continued her tales of sex for the older woman with her 2006 book "*Unaccompanied Women*". She wants "lots of sex with a man I like." [19]. The father of veteran crooner and heart-throb Julio Iglesias died of a heart attack shortly before he was to become a father for the second time in two years. The former gynaecologist, aged 90 and also called Julio, left his 42-year old wife expecting their second child in two years [20].

One of the seminal films of the 1960s, "*Belle de Jour*", was made by Spanish film director Luis Bunuel, at the age of sixty-six. British-born comic genius Charlie Chaplin was in films for over sixty years. He made "King in New York" at the age of 68, and had a young family when in his seventies. George Bernard Shaw, who also lived to a ripe old age, described ballroom dancing thus: "dancing is a perpendicular expression of a horizontal desire."

Chapter Ten

MOVING HOUSE

If you want to live in Spain, go for it.

Look at your house. Look at it now. Has it got two or three
stories? How steep are the stairs? And what about the
steps up to your house or up to your garage. Do you live on
a steep bank? Ok, you can manage these things perfectly
adequately now, but what about in ten or twenty years
time? Most of us at this stage in our lives want to stay in
the family home. It may be bigger than we actually need,
but it's nice to have plenty of space and to have a spare
bedroom or two to accommodate visitors, particularly
relatives. But what happens if you find in a few years time
that you can't manage all those stairs? Of course, you could
put in a stair lift, but is that really the answer? Lots of
people say that they would like to "retire" to a bungalow.
What I am saying is that, even if you are continuing to
work full time till your dying day, arthritis or other
physical debility might make it difficult for you to live
where you are now. Bungalows are the premium. Go and
look for one now, and buy it!

Let's think about the garden. Not long ago, I visited a
couple of old friends. They had retired to a very nice
bungalow, and it had a wonderful garden. Repeat: it had a
wonderful garden, but it wasn't so wonderful anymore. My
elderly friends were no longer able to manage this great big
garden by themselves, although they had been keen
gardeners throughout their lives. They would have been
happier with a much smaller garden, and one better

designed for their needs in later life. But it was too late, and they are now having to pay for someone to come and look after the garden for them. Of course they still enjoy the garden, but it's not quite the same as managing it yourself. So as well as looking for your ideal home later in life, you need to look for the ideal garden. For some, it will be no garden at all. As long as there are plenty of green spaces nearby with reasonable access and security, then do you really need to have a garden to yourself, one that you will either have to maintain yourself, or pay someone else to do so.

Granny Flat

This is fine, when it works. But have you ever stayed with your son/daughter since they lived with you as part of your family? Have you been on holiday together? Think about whether or not you are going to eat your meals together, watch television together, go shopping together. Sort out the ground rules – before the builders get to work. Decide who will contribute what to household costs, council tax, gas, water and electricity bills. Do you need a separate phone? And how often will you be expected to baby-sit your grandchildren? This could be where, and how, you will be spending the rest of your life. And can you really get on with your daughter-in-law or son-in-law, on a daily basis?

Moving to the seaside

For people who have never lived by the sea, and have only been to the seaside for holidays and day trips, moving to a seaside to live there permanently can be just as much a trauma as moving to another country. It's all very well thinking "we'll only be thirty miles away" from friends and family. Thirty miles can be a heck of a distance, especially if you are getting older and travelling is not so easy as it used to be. But the main thing is, remember you are cutting yourself off from friends and family and in some senses isolating yourselves from the life that you have led more or less since you were born.

Two close members of my family have "moved to the seaside" from the city, with differing results. My father's mother, Nana Wood, moved from the leafy suburbs of Chorlton-cum-Hardy to the shores of the Irish Sea at Lytham St Anne's. Although it was quiet and genteel and far removed in character from the popular and sometimes rowdy Lancashire seaside resort of Blackpool, just round the corner, it is at the seaside, just about. Now Nana Wood was a very keen golfer, and the presence of the Royal Lytham St Anne's golf course close by was undoubtedly an attraction. Lytham has nice shops, a quiet promenade, and the sea air. All that lasted Nana Wood about one week flat. When I cycled over to see her in her new abode for the first time, even as a teenager I realised that something was not quite right. Grandad Wood seemed ok. He was a champion bowls player, and was welcomed with open arms by the local bowls club. He slotted in straight away with his new male companions.

For my Nana, there was nobody. She did try the local WI and so forth, but no dice. She was a pushy, perky character who had her own decided views and did not easily adapt to others. In fact, she adapted not at all. As far as I recall, many of the cases were never unpacked and remained closed up until my grandparents could find a suitable home back in Chorlton. Nana said she missed her friends. Of course she did. In Chorlton, when she wanted to impress her opinions on one of her acquaintances, they could scarcely refuse. They had known her for years. But missing that background, she was completely incapable of making new connections. In addition, Lytham St Anne's is a fine and dandy place but it didn't quite have the cinemas and theatres that Manchester had, or even Chorlton for that matter. So just a few months after upping sticks and trekking over to Lytham, Nana and Grandad Wood moved back to Chorlton. They never moved again.

As a widow, Nana did try another move, this time to Grange-over-Sands, another genteel resort. Again, it just did not work. She decided to share a home with another widow – big mistake. Even as a teenager, I could see that there were problems with this arrangement, and not just because the house was up a very steep bank. Two women in the same kitchen just did not get on. It never was going to work. Both these ladies had been in total control of their own households for nearly half a century. They simply were not compatible. I believe her stay in Grange was even shorter than her stay in Lytham. Then it was back again to Chorlton, with my Dad taking on the role of long-suffering furniture remover.

An uncle and aunt of mine were a different kettle of fish. They also lived in Manchester, on a busy road. They were worried about their beloved dog getting run over. So they moved to a bungalow on a quiet estate on the North Wales coast, near the sea-front where they could walk the dog. Unfortunately, the dog died – of old age. Another couple we know moved to the South Coast, but complained that, whatever the time of year, there was always a chilly wind blowing. For all that you may have enjoyed your holidays by the sea enormously, if you're used to living inland, living by the sea all the year round may not be for you.

Moving abroad

This is a subject all of its own, and the subject of numerous books. It needs in-depth study to take account of your individual circumstances. Everyone is different, and what suits your friends might not suit you. Consider your health, your finances and find out in advance what services are available in the country of your choice. But if it suits you, go for it. Good luck!

Moving to Spain

This suits a lot of people. But it's still best to give it a try first. If you are going to stay in Spain all the year round, then just check out your chosen resort at different times of the year. Make sure there are plenty of activities to suit yourselves all year round. Then there's the question of what to do with your home back in the UK. Do you close it up and hope the burglars won't notice, empty it out or get some of your relatives to live in it, or sell it altogether? It's up to you. There are a lot of countries that you might want to go and live, but again it's a question of finding something that suits you, where you get on with the natives. It may well be that in Spain or wherever you can join an enclave of British folk. Fair enough. But you're bound to have contact with the natives, to a greater or less degree, so why not learn to speak their language? It could be fun, and it could lead to somebody different in you lives. Then when you want to travel to the hinterland, to see the "rural Spain" wherever you are, you'd be made much more welcome when you are asking directions in the locals' own language. Even if you are very bad at learning other peoples' languages.

Living in Spain

Quite a lot of people have gone to live in Spain and found it just ideal. They've found a place that suits them, amongst other people whose company they like, with the activities that they want to do. Brilliant. Fantastic. Couldn't be better. But that doesn't mean that living in Spain is for everybody. If you are thinking of a permanent move, surely it makes sense to go to that particular resort before you take the plunge. Go at different times of the year, and see how things are. In any case, you don't have to live in Spain all the time. You might want to live over there for so many weeks or months a year, if you can afford it. Selling the family home is quite something. As always, it will cost you that much more to buy the equivalent if you do decide to return. So think about these things. But if you really do want to, go and live in Spain,

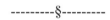

There has been an explosion of "grey pound" tourism. People aged 65 and over had been to an average of 12.8 countries, compared with just 5.8 for 18-25 year-olds, a survey has found. Four times as many people over-65 as under-35 had been to Morocco, while twice as many had been to South Africa, Kenya, New Zealand, Australia and Thailand [1]. A pensioner booked herself out of a retirement home because she found life there too dull. "It was full of old people with grey hair," complained Maria Milz of her time in Blankenheim, Germany. "I am a night owl." Frau Milz is 100 [2].

Chapter Eleven

WILLS, LIVING WILLS, POWER OF ATTORNEY

Making a will doesn't mean you'll die any sooner, but it will ease your mind.

I'm amazed at the number of people who don't make a will. Everybody should make a will. Most of all, make it absolutely clear what you want to happen. And make sure your will is somewhere where it can and will be found after your death. There's no point in making a will if it never comes to light. So leave a copy with your solicitor as well as in the house or with your nearest and dearest. You can always keep it sealed up to be opened after your death. Of course a will has to be witnessed and dated. Both are important to ensure that this is the genuine wish of the deceased person.

Your Living Will

This is something I would advise for every single senior citizen. We all have to die sometime, and once you pass sixty you realise that the number of years left for you is bound to be limited. Sooner or later we will all be incapacitated by accident or illness. But then it may be too late. We may not be able to express our preferences as to how we wish to be treated, and we will have no say over who makes those decisions for us. The great thing about making a living will is that not only do you dictate in advance how you want to be treated in your last months and weeks of life, but also who is to have the final say.

Power of Attorney

There are two types of power of attorney. One is signed by you in front of witnesses while you still have all your faculties. This type does not have to be registered, but allows another person, usually a close relative or trusted friend, to go to the bank or building society on your behalf and under your guidance. The other type is a registered power of attorney. Again, this is usually taken out by a close relative or trusted friend, usually when you have lost some faculties but can still instruct what needs to be done in the way of paying bills etc. Because it is registered, the person who becomes your representative has to keep written accounts of all monies spent on your behalf. It is probably better to have the first type when you are becoming physically frail but are still mentally alert. For the mentally frail, the second may be needed. A power of attorney can bring peace of mind both to you and to the friend or relative you want to act on your behalf.

We all have to die sometime

Yes, it's true. Even though most British people don't want to think about it, we all have to go sometime. I have been impressed by quite a number of old people that I have known over the years who have been philosophical about leaving this world. In fact some old people don't want to hang around. "I don't want to be a burden to anyone" is a common saying. Accepting that you are going to die at some point does not mean that you have to be morbid and miserable all the time. Far from it. Of course we are sad when someone we know and perhaps love dies. We know that we will no longer be able to enjoy their company and what they mean to us. But I feel that death may be the last full stop of the end of the last sentence of the last chapter of your last book, but it does not delete the book nor any of the books you have previously written.

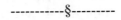

Four out of ten families now face paying inheritance tax. Ever-rising house prices have put forty-per cent of people above the £285,000 threshold for paying the tax. Fewer than half the people affected have taken any action to mitigate the effects of the tax, although more of the wealthy – those with estates valued at £2m or more – are using sophisticated tax loopholes to avoid paying [1]. A 94-year old woman declared dead sprang up and asked when Germany were next playing in the World Cup. When told she had been declared dead by doctors, Maria Muller said, "not likely, not until I see if Germany win the World Cup." [2].

Chapter Twelve

LIFESTYLE - CHOOSE YOUR OWN

Your life is yours to make of it what you will. And there's lots more years to come!

Remember, you want five portions of fruit and veg every day, that's easy to follow. Then avoid too much pre-processed food, cut down on salt, sugar and fat, then you won't go very wrong. Eat, drink and be merry – in moderation. A little bit of what you fancy does you good, so they say. But they do mean "a little bit".

Don't just eat to live

Of course when we are working and raising a family, there is very little time for anything. We have to eat as and when we can. Even if you continue this hectic lifestyle in your later age, it doesn't mean to say you have to eat junk. Of course food is fuel, but we are what we eat. And why not enjoy what you're eating? As well as making sure that what you eat makes you a better rather than a worse person.

And why not chew your food just that little bit more? I've lost quite a few teeth, but I'm hanging on to the ones I've got. This means I have to chew my food longer, but I'm sure that's all to the good. And there's no reason why a meal, any meal, shouldn't be some sort of occasion, either, whether you are eating by yourself or with someone else. I have little rituals, even when having a sandwich for lunch by myself. I will always have little preliminaries, and then follow things on in a certain order. This means that I can make meal times last a little bit longer, without actually eating too much. I'm not saying we should all be gourmets and live to eat, but don't just eat to live.

Keep taking the tablets

If you are on prescription drugs, as many of us are in older years, do take them regularly. Don't rely on someone else to remind you. You've helped to pay for the National Health Service – use it. Do have regular check-ups with the doctor or nurse at your local practice.

Frightened of the Doctor?

When I passed the age of sixty, I made up my mind to get a thorough check-up at the doctors. I drew up a list of questions. My wife added to the list and I took it along to the doctor. At one point in the conversation at the surgery, I did let out the information that I was having just a little trouble with my water-works - going a bit more often than normal, and not necessarily being able to empty the reservoir at every visit. A half smile played about the doc's lips. "Take your trousers off and get on the couch," he said. I didn't notice what he was doing behind his desk. Deliberately keeping it out of my gaze, he was putting on one of those surgical gloves. The test was over in seconds. I draw a veil over the details, but comedian Billy Connolly has made it a very graphic part of his stage act.

"Somewhat enlarged, but nothing to worry about at this stage," was my doctor's verdict. It seems that in gentlemen, our prostrate gland decides in the later years it's going to get bigger and bigger, thus blocking the ease of access of our urine via our urinary tract into the toilet bowl, hedge or whatever. This seems a bit unfair, but I suppose its something we have to put up with due to living so much longer. The thing is, it's a sort of macho feeling that we men have that stops us from going to see the doctor. "There's nothing wrong with me," or "don't worry, it'll wear off" is the sort of excuse men tend to make.

There it is, chaps, there's nothing macho about not going to the doctor. If there's something wrong with you, then go. Far better find out now rather than later. It's like the women with breast cancer. Better safe than sorry, and ignoring something won't in fact make it better. It can only get worse. And another thing: be honest with the doc. There's nothing he or she has not already seen, or heard. So tell him/her all your troubles. The one drawback I have found with all these visits to the doctors is the tests. Tests, tests and more tests. I am in a routine now. Down to the nurse, "have you come for your bloods?" is her cry. Yes, dear kind nurse, I have come for my bloods, or at least, yet another blood test. But if that's what it takes to keep me ticking along for a few more years, it's a small price to pay. As we are living longer, we all need to look after our bones and get our bone density checked. It's things like this that you need to put on the list to ask your doctor.

Learn to love your Dentist

Even harder than going down the doc's is going to the dentist. As with the doctor, there's absolutely nothing to gain in putting off a visit to the dentist. The sooner you go, the easier it will be both for you and your deontologist. Teeth never get better by themselves, they only get worse.

Give up smoking – it's never too late

There is simply no argument about the value of giving up smoking. Not only will it improve your own health and life expectations, it will also improve the health and life expectations of everyone else around you. And whatever age you give up, it will help you for your remaining years. One of the reasons I never started smoking was that I saw the agonies that my father went through trying to stop. He eventually did give up smoking altogether, but only after a terrible struggle. Once you're addicted, it's really tough to quit. But give up smoking, you must, for everyone's sake.

People often say to me, if everyone gave up smoking what would happen to the country's economy? The government depends so much on the vast amount of tax that we smokers pay. I have a complete answer to this specious argument. For a start, against the tax that cigarette smokers pay, there is the cost to the National Health Service of treating not only smokers but also the people who are affected by passive smoking, and that's a lorra, lorra people. They tell me that two thirds of the illnesses needing treatment by the NHS are caused by smoking, over-eating and over-indulgence in alcohol. There's also the cost of fires, particularly woodland fires caused by cigarettes, and cigarette smoking can also kill through fire.

Smoking Kills!

As a journalist I spent several years attending the local courts. Time after time I went to inquests where some person sadly died, in a fire, due to dropping a lighted cigarette either in a chair or sofa or in the bed. Sometimes there wasn't even a big fire, but smoke alone can kill without necessarily burning the house down. Smoke kills. Smoking kills, and smoking makes you very ill before it kills you. So don't do it. Oh yes, and another thing about the tax. If people didn't spend money on cigarettes, they would undoubtedly spend it on something else. Those goods and services would also generate jobs and tax revenue. So it's never a black-and-white case.

Any good at crosswords?

Crosswords are great for keeping the brain working. Remember, keeping the brain active is just as important as keeping the body active. For many people the daily crossword is a challenge and a joy. The satisfaction of completing it within a certain time can set you up for the day. For a change, try the code word puzzles where by you are given three or four letters of the alphabet and complete a crossword without clues. You might even try for the prizes that are on offer for crosswords. No reason why not. And now there's sudoku – addictive, isn't it? If you find crosswords do not suit you, there's lots of other puzzles which might suit your personality better – try them all. And you don't have to spend money on puzzle books, although they're usually quite cheap. Almost all newspapers now include a selection of puzzles to stretch the old grey matter.

Keep your brain alive

As with exercising your body every day, it's just as important to exercise your brain. Normal everyday conversations will do for a start, as will reading newspapers and magazines and taking some interest in the TV news or information programmes. Every so often I add up a column of figures by hand instead of using a calculator. I have to force myself to do it, as it's so much easier to use an electronic aid, but I need to make sure I can still do it. I've already mentioned that a daily crossword can be an excellent thing for keeping the brain sharp. And when there are quizzes either on the broadcast media or in print, then give them a go. Really try to see how much you can score and get some satisfaction from it. The internet is a great source of information. Set yourself a task to find something out, and really go for it. You can go online – usually for free – at your local Library. New information stimulates the brain. Talk to young people. They will challenge your accepted ideas, which can only be a good thing. And challenge your mates to remember things that happened in the past, a football match or a local event or whatever. You may get into arguments, but as long as they are friendly, that's no bad thing.

Take a nap!

Churchill did. When he was Prime Minister, Winston Churchill used to take a nap on a regular basis. He worked practically all round the clock, yet he was clearly up to the job of running the war. So if it's good enough for Winston Churchill, it's good enough for me. It's a fact that when we are older we don't sleep at night as we used to. We tend to wake up early and then get up rather than lie in bed, wide awake. No harm in that, especially if you can find something positive and active to do after breakfast. But I find that a few minutes' snooze just after dinner sets me up for the rest of the day. If I have to work right through lunch, I find myself flagging in the afternoon. The problem is, where to nap? At home, no problem. Elsewhere, it's a question of finding a comfy chair. From time to time, I have simply laid myself down on the ground and gone to sleep for a while. In a public place, there can be some danger attached to this, but if people can do it on the beach for example, then why not elsewhere? I have had people stop and look at me, and say "is he dead?" That's a small price to pay. The other place is in the cinema. They have such comfy seats now, virtually armchairs, that on some occasions I've found it very difficult to stay awake.

Sell the car?!?

You've got to be kidding! Sell the car? I couldn't possibly! Yes, in older age, sometimes you have to think the unthinkable. Most people get a car primarily to go to work. The car is also fantastically useful for going shopping, doing errands, going to films and football matches and so on, going on holiday, fetching and carrying of all kinds. To most people, a car is absolutely essential for life as it is lived. But if you have a restricted income and you no longer have to go to work or you have no job to go to, do you really, really need a car? Think about how many car journeys you have to take. Write down how much the car costs you to run, and I mean the full cost, included insurance, tax, fuel, depreciation, car parking charges and so forth. Reckon it all up, it must come to £2,000 a year at the very least.

Now consider the alternative. No car, walking, cycling, buses, trains and taxis. Yes, taxis. During the day, and for short journeys, taxis are relatively cheap and easy to get hold of. Why not budget for say two or three taxi journeys every week? Then add in your bus and train fares, remembering that us oldies can often get free or cut-price travel. For sometime now I've been travelling from the North East to London on a GNER train at £20 return fare. Fantastic! When I travel by coach, as I occasionally do, it's even cheaper. You can also get very cheap air-fares, so they tell me. But for most people that would mean getting to the airport by car. The point is, if your lifestyle does not absolutely require you to own and run a car, and if your income is limited, think about getting rid of it. You could even rent out the garage.

Many areas now give older people free or half fare travel passes. These are an enormous boon, and there's no reason why you shouldn't use them to the full. Having got rid of your car and saved yourself a lot of money, you can brag about it to the younger generation and tell them just how "green" you are and how you are helping the environment by taking your car off the road. They won't have any answer to that.

Holidays

Don't be rigid about holidays, unless it really suits your personality. Some people go to the same place at the same time of year every year for decades, and have a thoroughly good time. Nothing wrong with that whatsoever. But having a more flexible life in your later years means you can vary the pattern. You can go somewhere when it's cheaper. You can take more holidays. You can take longer holidays, but you can also take shorter ones, weekend breaks, a day away. There's just about every possible form of holiday to choose from, from a coach trip to a round-the-world cruise. Pick something that's within your budget and which has some element that you'll be sure will give you some enjoyment. Don't get stuck on a cruise which doesn't suit you. It must be terrible handing out a four-figure sum to find you're stuck on a boat where the activities do not suit you. Some people absolutely love cruises, some people loathe them. The same thing applies to canal boat trips. Try it for a short while first, before you book a fortnight's cruise.

Be careful who you take on holiday. If you have not been on holiday with your relatives or friends before, be absolutely certain that you will still be speaking to each other at the end of the holiday. Make sure you all have your own space just in case there are clashes and arguments, as so often can be the case. Again, it's really horrible if you booked a chalet, a caravan or a canal boat for a fortnight, only to find you've had a terrific row with your companions after only the third day. Also, think about the weather. Be prepared for inclement weather, especially if holidaying in the UK. The thing to do is to have activities in mind or places to go when the weather is bad, rather than just sitting and moping around. The worst kind of holiday I can think of is where you are always thinking "what can we do to fill in the time?" It shouldn't be a case of filling in time till lunch, filling in time till tea, and so on. That is wasting your life. The way I look at it, I may only have a few years left, and I'm damn certain I'm not going to fritter them away by "filling in time".

And don't be afraid of doing your own thing. Not only do we all need our own space, getting away from your partner from time to time can and does in most cases enhance and strengthen your relationship, not weaken it. Remember "absence makes the heart grow fonder." And it follows that spending time apart, particularly for two very different individuals, can also be a boon. So take it sensibly. The same sort of rules could be applied even to a humble shopping expedition. One partner can go off to one shop, the other to another. Most parents nowadays like their teenage children to have a mobile phone with them so that they can be contacted and that the youngsters can contact their parents if they are in any kind of trouble. That is a great comfort to both. The same applies to older people who are out on the town, whether shopping or otherwise.

Keep your own space

Now I know there are couples, happily-married couples, that like nothing better than to be in each other's company. However, for blokes who've had their own offices and work spaces for all their working lives, it is a culture shock to have to give all that up to share what has been mainly their partner's domain for a couple of decades, probably since the kids left. For a lot of couples, as long as a man has the cellar, the attic, his own "study", a greenhouse or – best of all – his shed, then all is well. The male of the species can disappear into his little corner and do his own thing at his own pace in his own time to his own content, leaving his partner happy and healthy and still boss lady of the remainder of the premises. He is in his own little world free on constraints, and she "knows where he is". That's a great formula. Discuss this issue well before the date of your retirement comes along. But make sure you've got your own space to pursue your hobby. Consider buying a shed, if you haven't already got one. Or it may be a good idea to convert the loft.

The same can and often should apply when you go on holiday. I am all for those couples who completely share their interests on holiday, and do everything together. But it may be that one prefers shopping to golf and vice versa. Parting for an hour or two to meet up later in the day to resume your mutual interests can be a boon. As long as you both completely understand the time and place where you are to meet, and how you are to communicate if the arrangement falls though, then all is well. In this respect I can thoroughly recommend the mobile telephone.

There's nothing more frustrating than turning up at the appointed time and place only to find that your loved one is not there and there is no means of communicating with him or her. That way lies disagreement, unhappiness and potentially divorce − all devoutly to be avoided at any time, but most of all in your later years.

No shame in having a cleaner

Almost all women are house-proud. Even men now, particularly in their later years, are taking to doing a bit of housework. Most people would be horrified about the idea of having someone else to come in and clean. But what's wrong with having a little help around the house, particularly if you are finding it difficult to do it yourself? Why wait until you're so incapacitated that you have to have a home help and go the whole hog as it were? Look at your budget, and if you need the help and you can afford it, then do it. There's no shame in that whatsoever. The same applies to the garden. Just getting the grass cut and/or the weeding done by someone else, whether paid or not, leaves you time to do the planting etc.

Go green - recycle

Pay a visit to your local recycling centre. You could be in for a pleasant surprise. I'm all for these centres being run by what I see as very capable entrepreneurs. These lads and lasses really sort out your junk, and if they find something that's re-saleable, well good luck to them. You can congratulate yourself on reducing the amount of waste that simply goes into a hole in the ground. Although it may still be the cheapest option in many ways, it is the least friendly way of disposing of the things we don't need. I can now give myself a pat on the back because, most time I go to the supermarket, I take two or three supermarket bags with me and reuse them, rather than accumulating hundreds at home. And I'm a regular at the paper, can and bottle banks. I even keep a spare cardboard container for the bottles of wine. I must tell you, this gives you lots and lots of brownie points and makes you feel so superior about helping the environment.

As a society we have yet to catch on to proper recycling. We are making progress with regard to recycling fridges and cars, but electrical equipment is still a no-go area. Eventually we will realise that we cannot go on indefinitely making things and simply disposing of them when they are no longer any use to us. Instead of forgetting all about what happens after we have finished with something, we ought to think of the life of a television for example, as a complete cycle, whereby when it has completed its useful life its bits go back into the system to be reused in some way or another. Surely that's the only way we can save the planet, but it needs a change of mental attitude. If all us older citizens really went to town on recycling, what a difference that would make. I've always found youngsters keen and eager to learn about recycling and protecting the environment. It's just the adults inbetween who are the problem. So let's get to it, make allies of our grandchildren, and get everybody recycling.

Get rid of the rubbish

Even those houses that look neat as a new pin will have stuff hidden away in the attic or in sheds. Get rid of it! When you die, they'll simply bring along a van and cart it all away to the nearest tip. If you are in serious need of de-cluttering your house, get a few books on the subject from the Library. At least this will give you some good ideas on how to psyche yourself up to begin the task. Taking it slowly but surely could possibly keep you busy for at least a year. Then, when your house is sufficiently de-cluttered and there are no longer any excuses left to prevent you doing all those other things you know you should be doing, book yourself in at the local College to learn a new hobby – and start cluttering up your house all over again!

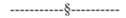

DVLA (Driver and Vehicle Licensing Agency) figures show 34 people over 100 years of age in the UK held a valid driving licence in 2005. Figures for other older drivers: 96-100 years (1,555 UK drivers), 91-95 yrs (21,405), 86-90 yrs (121,694), 81-85 yrs (453,773), 76-80 yrs (844,043). That's nearly one and a half million drivers aged seventy-six and over [1]. Japan's "super elderly" are healthier, more active and more numerous than ever. Japan has over 25,000 centenarians, one in 5,000 of the population. In Okinawa, one person in 2,000 is over 100. Japan celebrates "Respect the Aged Day" [2].

"The chief joy of reaching my prime is that I couldn't care less what anybody thinks or says about me" – journalist and writer Bel Mooney. "Instead of saying 'one door closes, another opens', you fling open ALL the doors. The truth is, never before have I felt such a powerful passion for life. We baby-boomers are surely the luckiest generation. Born in 1946, we imbibed post-war relief and optimism with our mothers' milk, and experience a safe and structured childhood during the undervalued 1950s." [3].

Sixty-year olds have been renamed GOTYs – Getting Older, Thinking Younger – by social and economic analysts who say that many 60-year olds feel in the prime of life and are "ageing positively". Research into the biggest and wealthiest consumer group in Britain says life has never been better for those over fifty. They hold 80 per cent of the country's wealth. 49 per cent of over-fifties enjoy an active sex life [4].

A study in Holland of men aged 70-80 found mental performance fell three and a half times more quickly in those who were inactive, compared with active men. Physical activity is thought to improve blood flow to the brain, reducing the risk of stroke and dementia, and also improving memory [5]. In 2007, veteran entertainer Danny La Rue OBE was making his comeback at smaller venues after recovering from a minor stroke, aged eighty [6].

In 2005, 66-year old former restaurateur Patricia Tabram was facing a possible jail term after admitting possession of a drug with intent to supply. She had been cooking cannabis casseroles for her friends in the village of Humshaugh, near Hexham in Northumberland, as a natural remedy for tinnitus, mild depression and aches and pains caused by a car crash [7]. Primary schoolchildren in 1956 featured in a black and white teacher-training film "Free to grow". The kids are shown doing exercise, including gymnastics, skipping, hula-hooping and dance –

and not one of the pupils shown is overweight. Chances are that most if not all of the class at New Earswick, near York, are still fit and healthy fifty years later [8].

Crime thriller writer Raymond Chandler, who created the fictional private eye Philip Marlowe and wrote "*The Big Sleep*" and "*Farewell my Lovely*", died in 1959 aged seventy-one. His last book "*Playback*" was published the year before.

Chapter Thirteen

OPTIMISTS ENJOY LIFE MORE

This is true!

Yet we are grumpy, we old people. There's so much in the modern world to be grumpy about. For a start, take technology. I think there's something in my genes that stops me from appreciating technology of all kinds, but particularly new technology. My great-grandfather ran his own press agency on virtually the same lines as I came to do a century later, without realising that I was in fact replicating what my ancestor had done. Great-grandad operated through a network of correspondents, exactly as I did, but the main thing was, he did not like new technology. My great-grandfather refused to use the typewriter or the telephone, even though they had been invented. He saw absolutely no reason why he should not continue to use his "dippy-in" pen to write his stuff, and the Post Office Telegraph to receive information from his correspondents and to send out his finished articles to the various newspapers that he worked for: just like me.

Yes, I did use the typewriter (and now a computer keyboard), and the telephone (now with the addition of a mobile phone), but the only reason I started using a computer to type up my copy was when my last typewriter finally broke down and I couldn't find another one anywhere in the world. Even the Czechs had stopped making typewriters. So I reluctantly moved onto a computer. Mind, I now swear by these computers. They're great for getting your material into good order, and better still for the "copy and paste" system, a boon to freelance journalists like me. But the point is that both great-grandfather and I were reluctant to give up our tried and tested methods of doing business and move on to something new. He was a laggard and I am definitely one too.

I hear what you say, what is a laggard? Well, if you have done the Open University like what I have, you would have learnt that in society there are the innovators, the majority and the laggards. The innovators are always keen to try the latest, well, innovation. When they have proved it to be a success, the majority follow suit. The last few stragglers who finally and reluctantly come on board with everyone else are the laggards. I can see some far distant ancestor of ours in the Stone Age or whatever who was quite happy to go hunting animals with spears, for example. I have read that some early two-legged creature went for half a million years or more stabbing his prey with a spear. Every time this particular early man went hunting, he put his life in danger by having to stab his intended prey from close quarters. Then along comes some new bright Stone Age youth who says to him: "Grandad, here's a great new system. Instead of stabbing from close quarters, all you have to do is to throw the spear from a safe distance. It's just as effective, but it keeps you well away from the beast who may lash out with tooth and claw when you are next door to him, stabbing him the meanwhile."

But our elder ancestor undoubtedly turned to this young whippersnapper and said: "Look, stabbing animals from close quarters has been a tried and trusted method for me, my father, my grandfather and so on for the last half a million years. You don't expect me to change now. In any case, at least if you stab something you can hardly miss it from three feet away. Your idea of throwing spears from a distance looks very dodgy to me. You could easily miss, and then where would you be? Besides, when you're stabbing something, you can stab it several times. Whereas, your new-fangled method of throwing a spear gives you one chance and one chance only of striking a fatal blow. No, close-quarter stabbing is good enough for me and I'm not going to change." Fortunately, the innovators proved that their system was better, and so mankind progressed to the pinnacle of civilisation as we know it today. The moral of this story is, recognise yourself what you are. Be happy in your own skin. You don't have to change.

All-singing, all-dancing Mobile Phones

There's no law that says you have to adopt the latest gadget, such as these all-singing, all-dancing mobile phones. Mobile phones, there's another thing. Whereas I always book my seat on GNER from Darlington to King's Cross in the quiet coach and look askance at anyone breaking that rule, I must admit that having a mobile phone is a necessity of modern life, for me at least. If you can still manage without one, then good luck to you. But it's rather like being without a television. It's only for the very, very fanatical few.

The only thing I would say to mobile phone latecomers is, get the best deal you can. When you sign up for a mobile phone, you are usually offered umpteen hours of free calls. Don't take them. If you do, you will find yourself making any amount of useless calls. You will waste loads of your valuable time and chatting away vacuously over the airwaves to no purpose whatsoever, upsetting your friends and relatives and doing yourself no good at all. If teenagers want to fill up their time with useless chatter, then so be it. It's a free country. Far better get a deal whereby your basic monthly charge is less with a modest number of so-called "free" minutes. Because, like everything else, when you take these new gadgets on board, they usually cost something extra, if not a lot extra. So just watch the bills. Remember, the cost of your mobile phone is over and above your regular telephone or land-line as we experts call it, and not instead of. You could scratch the land-line altogether, something I would not recommend, but it might work for you.

Computer course

Something I would recommend is to go on a computer course. When you buy one of these fairly expensive gadgets, it will undoubtedly come with the ability to do millions of things: millions. All I want to use a computer for is (a) as a glorified typewriter, and (b) as a source of information. But it does make sense for you to learn just what you can do with your computer, and if there are other things that you would like to do with it, play music and so forth, then that's all to the good. But try going on a course, and there are lots and lots of courses, quite a lot at little cost and some at no cost at all, then go to it. It also might be a way of meeting people and widening your horizons.

It's taken me a long time to get round to the main point of grumpy old men and that is you may be grumpy, but just be grumpy to yourself and not to the world at large. Even your dear wife, and certainly your relatives, friends, etc, do not want to know about your ailments. I know this is a major topic of conversation amongst people of a certain age, and I could give you a complete encyclopaedia of my internal problems, rather on the lines of Jerome K Jerome in his fantastically funny tome "*Three Men in a Boat*" ie everything except Housemaid's Knee, but I won't.

119

Just think about this for a moment. When you meet another person of older age, man or woman, do you want to hear about their ailments and health problems? No, you do not. Nor do they want to hear about yours. Now there may be a rich vein of conversation with regard to the ills of the world at large. We all railed against the injustices of governments at all levels and the stupidity of those set in authority above us. Not to say what we think of the younger generation and all their daft goings on.

Just remember, every single generation throughout history has bemoaned the next generation coming on after it, and the one after that. So if you want to do it, and you can find someone else to share your thoughts on that particular topic, then go ahead. But if you want to communicate with the younger generation, for heavens sake don't tell them what a load of rubbish they are, they might tell you the same thing.

Enjoy the past, don't live in it

To be fair, I don't think there are too many people who just live in the past. Not like that Miss Haversham in Dickens' novel "*Great Expectations*". Actually, somebody has worked out that Miss Haversham could not be more than forty-five years of age. Never mind, it's a great tale. It seems to me that far too many people nowadays want to forget about the past and in some instances obliterate it from their minds and lives altogether. Now that can't be a good thing. What you are now is an accumulation of everything that has happened to you from the moment you were born, and probably a good deal before that. They do say that when you get married, you should look at your new spouse and then at their appropriate parent. In other words, in twenty to twenty-five years time, the bride will look like her mother and the groom like his father. This may be true, but you don't necessarily have to replicate that.

The whole person

What I'm after is for each of us to recognise ourselves as a whole person with a complete history. I'm proud of what I am, and I recognise that what I am is an accumulation of my personal and family history, the circumstances of my birth, upbringing and the life I have led under my own steam as an adult. In a sense, I don't regret anything that has happened to me, not even the bad parts. For a start, the bad parts have still had an effect on your character and personality as they are now. Without the bad parts, how can you enjoy the good parts?

This is easier for me, as I was brought up very much on the basis of PEDR (the Protestant Ethic of Deferred Reward). To put it another way, no gain without pain. So even the pain is helpful, looking back on it. They do say that some of the young men and women in the Victorian era who had been born into great wealth and never ever had a job or a role in life, actually went mad. With no objective, their whole lives were simply filling in time. Far better to be born a little lower down the scale and have to struggle for what you get. This is so much more in line with the way that we are built. We were made to struggle.

I know plenty of older people who take quiet pride in the fact that they came through the war, brought up a family, set their children on their way in life, held down a job for most of their lives and built up a home and possessions. Now what's wrong with that? As long as we continue to look to the future and how we may make the most of our lives, there's nothing wrong with looking back on what you've done in your life.

Step down happily

Some people never know when to quit. They go on and on, well past their "sell-by" date, damaging themselves as well as everyone else. So many people who have made a successful transition from one lifestyle to another say that it's better to quit at the top or at least while you are still ahead. Family firms are a case in point. For a man in particular who has built up a business and been very successful, it's extremely hard to take a back seat and to put his "baby" in the hands of his human offspring, very, very, hard. But it is necessary, not only for the health of the business but also for the health and wellbeing of the original entrepreneur.

I see this done very successfully in the farming community. Farmers are by their very nature and experience strong-minded individuals, used to battling officialdom, the elements, the markets and so on. Yet I am happy to say that I have seen frequent examples where a farmer has happily and easily handed on to his next generation. Dad and mother are still there, living nearby, ready to give a hand or even to give advice – but only when asked. Everyone needs to make their own mistakes. It is a wise man or woman who realises that the best thing they can do for their children is to set them away to make their own course in life. As I say, we all have to make our own mistakes. Most of the time, the transition is successful. And think how satisfying it must be to the older generation to see their offspring succeeding in their own way, adapting to new and every changing circumstances.

Yes, you do have wisdom

Be confident in yourself. You have a lifetime's experience. For all that most of that experience was years ago, it still counts. The principles of business have not changed very much. Human nature has not changed at all. So, yes, be confident that you do have something to offer the younger generation. The trick is, to avoid being seen to dictate or to run things yourself. Ideally, you should only give your advice when asked. By all means offer it, but always make sure that you are suggesting an alternative rather than criticising any current activities of your juniors who are now responsible for running things. We all go through the traumas of youth and of parenthood, so it can be very reassuring to be able to tell your son/daughter or grandson/ granddaughter that they are not the first person to suffer the pangs of unrequited love, of a break-up, or have offspring who have gone the wrong way.

There are many uses for your wisdom beyond your immediate family. There are many local organisations that would welcome your help in some capacity. If you have had experience in the world of finance, so many organisations are crying out for a treasurer or an auditor to help them keep their accounts straight. Many organisations are involved in making applications for grants. Here again, you may have the know-how that will help them along. And you will get a great deal of satisfaction from doing so.

Always look on the bright side

Monty Python gave us many things, and for me one of their outstanding creations has been the song "*Always Look on the Bright Side of Life*" as sung by the people being crucified by the Romans in their satirical film *"The Life of Brian"*. To some, it is a bit sickening for this extremely cruel form of execution to be made fun of. Everyone who was crucified died in agony. Many took hours to die, some even days. But Monty Python has shown us a very great truth. We always have something to be thankful for. Of course we would all wish to avoid unnecessary pain and suffering, of a far lesser degree than crucifixion.

I am fortunate in that, apart from occasional visits to the dentist, I have not suffered any really serious physical pain. Perhaps that is still to come. I have suffered a lot of mental and emotional anguish and turmoil, which to me was just as bad if not worse. During the black days of my long-drawn-out divorce, I woke up every day with a pain that seemed to be truly physical. I carried that pain with me for months on end. But I was able to tell myself that it would eventually go away, and so it did.

I've no wish to make light of bereavement, nor of other things that do happen to us. But in the absence of a sincere religious belief, I would suggest that mankind has a natural inborn optimism that things can and will get better. If we do not suffer pain, whether physical or emotional, then how can we appreciate it to the full when things are better? I cannot imagine a life without any of the downside, it just would not seem natural or truly satisfying to me.

So "Always Look on the Bright Side of Life" is a grand motto to have, whatever your age.

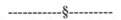

Scientists have discovered "Irritable Male Syndrome", the male equivalent of PMS (pre-menstrual tension). Dr

Gerard Lincoln of the Medical Research Council's reproductive science unit in Edinburgh said, "IMS happens when testosterone levels decline. This can make men emotional, nervous and fractious, as well as lowering their self-esteem." [1]. Approaching 71, "pop's greatest living icon" [greatest living rocker, surely – CFW] Jerry Lee Lewis is still strutting his stuff on stage. Off-stage, he was recently divorced from his sixth wife and has a history of booze and drug abuse that would have finished off many less determined men years ago [2].

Bertha Wood, who ran a Blackpool holiday camp, has published her memoirs *"Fresh Air and Fun"* at the age of 100, She is in the *"Guinness Book of Records"* as the oldest published first-time author [3].

When Arthur Best of Worthen in Shropshire turned ninety, he placed a bet of £110 with William Hill at odds of 66/1 that he would live to be 100. In January 2005 he collected his winnings of £7,370 to help his centenary birthday celebrations. French actress Sarah Bernhardt had a leg amputated when she was seventy but still carried on with her stage career until she died eight years later. Actress Dame Edith Evans made her first film at the age of sixty. At 75, Clint Eastwood won two Oscars in 2005 for his film *"Million Dollar Baby"* for best film and best producer. Oh, and he acted in the film as well.

Chapter Fourteen

THE LAST WORD - ENJOY YOUR LIFE

Have you been listening?

I hope this book has helped you to think positively. Whatever our personal beliefs, we have this one time on earth - so let's make the most of it! All the very best for the future, as long or as short as it may be. CFW.

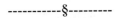

Sophia Loren has been voted the world's most naturally beautiful person at the age of 71. She is to feature in the 2007 Pirelli calendar [1]. Actress Jane Fonda, 68, signed a six-figure deal to be the face of L'Oreal Paris anti-ageing cream. Forty years after bursting onto the scene as a Sixties teenage model, Twiggy has again been a smash as a model for Marks and Spencer. But she's only 56 [2].

Still beautiful, French film actress Catherine Deneuve, 62, is to be the face of MAC Cosmetics [3]. British actress Joan Collins, still glamorous at 72, is to launch her first ever UK tour [4]. At 60, Roxy Music frontman Bryan Ferry was taken on by Marks and Spencer as a male model, photographed by David Bailey. He joins sixties model Twiggy and veteran rocker Mick Jagger in a new marketing campaign as M&S revives its fortunes [5.

Film star Gina Lollobrigida, once hailed as the most beautiful woman in the world, announced her latest marriage in 2006. She was 79, her husband-to-be a 45 year-old estate agent [6]. Jazzman Jay "Hootie" McShann from Oklahoma had a 75-year professional career. Starting in 1931, the pianist, singer, bandleader and composer played jazz, blues, boogie-woogie, ballads and R'n'B, but always in the swinging style associated with Kansas City. He was still swinging at 90 [7].

Nancy Pelosi has brought "glitz and glamour" to Washington as the first woman Speaker of the House of Representatives, third in line to the president. She was described as looking "powerful, tasteful and chic" in her Giorgio Armani suit. A mother of five and grandmother of six, Mrs Pelosi is 66 [8]. Writer Christabel Burniston published her latest novel "The Brass and the Velvet" at the age of 90 [9].

1001 THINGS TO DO

ABSEILING
  No age limit
  For charity
AGE CONCERN
  Volunteers welcome
AGRICULTURAL SHOWS
  Visit
  Exhibit
  Sell your product
ALLOTMENTS
  Flowers
  Fruit
  Vegetables
AMATEUR DRAMATICS
  Act
  Costumes
  Make-up
  Produce
  Direct
  Sound
  Front of house
  Write
AMAZON
  Buy
  Sell
  Business
ANTIQUES
  Collect
  Buy
  Sell

Write articles
Go on tv
ARCHAEOLOGY
  Go on a dig
  Study
  Classify
  Report
  Discover
  Preserve the past
  Treasure trove
ARCHERY
  Join a club
ARTS ASSOCIATION
  Join one
  Start one
ASTROLOGY
  Serious study
  Fun
ASTRONOMY
  Buy a telescope
  Visit an observatory
  Discover new objects
ATHLETICS
  Keeping fit
  Little brother, big sister
  Compete at any age
  Clubs & coaching
  Orienteering
  Cross-country
  Fun runs

Marathons
Half marathons
Triathlon
Biathlon

BADMINTON
Join a club
BALLET
A theatre experience
BANDS
Brass
Silver
Rock
BEER
Real Ale
Visit pubs
Visit breweries
Make your own
BEACH-COMBING
Shells
Flotsam
Valuable items
BEREAVEMENT
Cruse (charity)
Counselling
BILLIARDS
Still popular
BINGO
Fun & prizes
Socialise
Make new friends
Share your winnings
Be a caller!
BIRD WATCHING

Hides
Be a twitcher
Recording
Feeding
Rescuing
BLUE BADGE
Know your area
Be a guide
Earn money
Meet people
BOARD GAMES
All ages can play
Use your old ones
Buy new ones
BOATS
Yachts
Cruisers
Speedboats
Racing
Water skiing
BUSES
Use that bus pass!
Travel the country
Try new services
First and last journeys
Buy your own bus
Drive a community bus
BROADCASTING
Local radio
Hospital radio
Phone-ins

CAMPING
  Solo
  Two-person
  Families
  Basic
  Luxurious
  Cheap
  Lightweight tents
  Facilities of choice
CANALS
  Walk
  Fish
  Canal Boats
  Holidays
  Sight-seeing
  Help restore
CANOEING
  Safety first
  Join a club
  Competition
  White-water
CARDS
  Card games
  Bridge
  Poker
  On-line gaming
  Whist drives
CARERS
  Being one
  Having one
CARPENTRY
  Absorbing hobby
  Paying hobby

CARS
  Maintain
  Repair
  Veteran
  Vintage
  Shows
  Exhibitions
  Racing
  Rallying
CATTLE
  Smallholding
  Selling meat, milk
  Competitions
  Showing stock
  Breed Societies
CHARITIES
  Helping
  Working
  Organising
  Fund raising
  Sponsored events
CHARITY SHOPS
  Volunteers always
    wanted
CHESS
  Clubs
  By post
CHOIRS
  Very satisfying
  Good social side
  Travel
  Appreciative audiences
  Making records

CHRISTMAS CARDS
  Edit that Christmas list
  Make your own
  Christmas Letter
CHURCH
  Men's groups
  Women's groups
  Lead a youth group
  Join the choir
  Lay preacher
  Become a minister
  Flower rota
  Sidesmen/women
CLASSIC CARS
  Associations
CLIMBING
  Learn the ropes!
COLLECTING
  Compelling hobby
  Try something different
  The world is your oyster
  Plan
  Specialise
  Find space
  Join a club
  Budget
  Make collecting pay
  Buying
  Selling
COMMUNITY BUS
  Support your local group
  Be a driver
COMPUTERS
  The universe on line

Window to the world
  Many courses
  Learn
  Teach
  Write
  Print
COSTUME
  Join the Society
COUNCILLORS
  Get elected
  County
  Borough
  District
  Town
  Parish
  Community
  Chairman
  Mayor
COUNSELLING
  Help others
COURTS
  Free entertainment
  Major trials
  Fascinating
CRAFTS
  Learn
  Pass on knowledge
  Tradition
CRICKET
  Join a club
  Playing member
  Social member
  Committee member
  Ground staff

In the park
On the beach
French cricket

CROCHET
Anywhere
Any time

CROSS-COUNTRY
RIDING
Competition

CROSS-COUNTRY
RUNNING
Veterans competition

CROSSWORDS
Every standard
Books to help

CUB SCOUTS
Boys & girls
Be a leader

CYCLING
Get the right bike
Stay safe
Social
Competition
Clubs
Coaching
Holidays
Touring
Cyclo-cross
Track racing
Time-trialling
Tricycles
Tandems
Vintage
Historic

DANCE
Classes near you
Something for everyone
Keeping fit
Expand your social life
Dress up
Look/feel glamorous

DANCING
Ballroom
Jive
Salsa
Tango
Flamenco
Samba
Line
Belly
Break
Tap
Country

DARTS
Usually in pubs
Women too

DIETING
Change your habits
Enjoy food
Exercise
No yo-yo dieting
Realistic targets
Family support

DISCRIMINATION
Equality Commission

DIVING
Springboard
High

Sub-Aqua
DOMINOES
Cut-throat competition
DRAMA
Watch
Participate
DRAUGHTS
Not so innocent
Fierce competition
DRESS
Try something new
Dress up
Dress down
Please yourself!
Make your own clothes
DRESSMAKING
Useful skill
Learn
Teach
DRINKING
The Great British Pub
Know your limits
Drinking & driving (not)
Drinking at home
Wine tasting
Visit the vineyards
Brew your own beer
Make your own wine
Alcohol dependence –
warning signs
DRIVING
Car maintenance
Take people out
Plan your route

DRUMS
Orchestra
Band
Group
Social

EATING OUT
Experiment
Learn the ropes
Choosing the wine
Tipping
Complaining
EBAY
Buy & sell
Make money
EQUALITY
Equality Commission
ENTERTAINING
Sing
Dance
Tell jokes
Play music
Ready audiences

FAMILY HISTORY
Endless fascination
Thrill of the search
Finding "lost" relatives
Travel with a purpose
Interviewing techniques
Building a family tree
For future generations
Photos
Tapes

Videos
Family History Societies
FINANCE
Check yours
Taking your pension
Investments
Investment Clubs
Budgeting
Downsize your home
Insulate – more warmth,
  less cost
Utilities (gas etc) – shop
  around
Turn unwanted items
  into cash
Do you really need a car?
FIRST AID
Red Cross
St John's Ambulance
Scouts
Guides
Learn
Teach
Attend events
FISHING
Most popular particip-
  ation sport
Rivers
Ponds
Lakes
Sea fishing
Competition
FITNESS
Choose any activity

FLYING
Fixed wing planes
Helicopters
Jet planes
Gliders
Hot-air balloons
Microlites
FLOWER ARRANGING
Courses
Church rota
FOLLOW THE STARS
Join the fans
Collect autographs
Memorabilia
Get to know your
  favourites
Join a fan club
Run a fan club
FOOTBALL
Over-forties leagues
Five-a-side soccer
Coaching
Refereeing
Club official
Support your local team
Always a fan
Ground-hopping
FRETWORK
Absorbing hobby
Useful objects
FRIENDS REUNITED
Old Boys reunions
Old Girls reunions

Join the OB/OG
  Association
See how they turned out
Meet an old flame
FUNERALS
  Do go

GAMBLING
  The Lottery
  Scratch cards
  On-line gaming
  Find the Lady
  Casinos
  Las Vegas
  Monaco
  Manchester
GAME SHOWS
  Get on the telly!
  Be prepared
  Combine your skills
GARDENING
  Satisfying, absorbing
  Hobby
  Pastime
  Passion
  Use your garden
  Low maintenance garden
  The perfect lawn
  Fruit
  Flowers
  Vegetables
  Exhibit
  Garden club
  Leek club

Flower Society
GOATS
  Run a smallholding
  Sell meat, milk & cheese
  Competitions
  Show your stock
  Breed Societies
GRANDPARENTS
  Babysit
  Enjoy your grandchildren
  Join an Association
GREETINGS CARDS
  Edit Christmas list
  Make your own
  Christmas Letter
  Birthdays
  Weddings
  Anniversaries
  Good luck
  Get well
  Condolences
GUIDES
  Be a leader
GYMNASTICS
  Stay supple
  Trampolining
  Coaching

HAIRDRESSING
  Try a new style
  Hairdressing at home
  Learn
  Practice on friends/family
  Earn

HANG-GLIDING
  Paragliding
HEALTH
  Eating to live
  Enjoy your food
  Lose weight
  Enjoyable exercise
  Think long-term
  Active in mind/body
HERITAGE
  Help save it
HIKING
  Good boots essential
  Solo
  Social walking
  Healthy
  Countryside
  Holidays
HOCKEY
  Mixed teams
  Join the club
  Running a team
  Official
  Administrator
HOME HELPS
  Be one
HORSE RIDING
  Take lessons
  Keeping a horse
  Pony
  Dressage
  Show jumping
  Cross-country
  Eventing

Trekking
Riding abroad
HORSES
  Competitions
  Showing
  Breed societies
HOSPITAL VISITOR
  Just enquire
HUNTING
  Ride
  On Foot
  Follow
  Hounds
HURLING
  Watch
  Coach

ICE HOCKEY
  Watch
  Coach
ICE SKATING
  Social
  Competitive
  Shows
ILLNESS
  Face the truth
  Positive helps healing
  Don't be a bore
INDUSTRIAL
 ARCHAEOLOGY
  Choose your industry
INTERNET
  Many courses
  Ultimate information

Broadband
Business
Buying
Selling
Amazon
Ebay
Your own website
Write a Blog
Help others
INVESTMENT CLUBS
Free advice
Pool investments
Social side

JIGSAWS
Absorbing hobby
Solo or joint
Make your own
JOURNALISM
Articles
Local correspondent
Letters to the Editor

KNITTING
Anytime, anywhere

LIFELONG LEARNING
See web
LOCAL HISTORY
Many societies
Start one
Collect material
Archive

Preserve the past for the
future
LISTED BUILDINGS
Check in your area
Report conditions
Help restore
LUNCH CLUBS
Help

MAGIC
Learning
Social
Amateur
Professional
The Magic Circle
Watch & learn
MAKE-UP
Theatre
MARTIAL ARTS
Learn
Teach
MEALS ON WHEELS
Cook
Driver
MEMORABILIA
Collect
MENSA
Take the test
MODEL-MAKING
Choice of thousands
MOTOR CYCLES
Don't kill yourself
MOUNTAINEERING
Know the rules

MUSEUMS
See the changes
Inter-active
Great to visit
Be a guide
MUSIC
Listen
Play
Bands
Orchestras
Quartets
Jazz
Classical
Country
Folk
Rock
Directing

NAIL CARE
Treat yourself
Paying hobby
NATIONAL TRUST
Visit sites
Become a Member
Volunteer Warden
NEEDLEWORK
Absorbing
Learn
Teach
NEIGHBOURHOOD WATCH
Community safety
Special constables
Street wardens

NETBALL
Coach
Official
NEW DEAL 50 PLUS
See website
OPEN UNIVERSITY
Learn at home
ORIENTEERING
Great fun
OVER-SIXTY CLUBS
Look in

PAINTING
For pleasure & profit
Oils
Water colours
Exhibiting
PARACHUTING
No age limit
PARISH & TOWN COUNCILS
Council meetings
Parish meetings
Petitions
Formation
PARLIAMENT
See your MP, MEP, House
  of Lords member
Visit, watch & listen
See your Councillor
PEDICURE
Look after your feet
Treat yourself
PENSIONER POWER

Visit
Travel
RAMBLERS
  Local Groups
  National Association
READ
  Fiction
  Non-Fiction
  Reading for pleasure
  Use your library
RED CROSS
  Learn
  Teach
  Attend events
RELIGION
  Act on your beliefs
RESEARCH
  Resume your studies
  Experiments
  Scientific papers
RIDING
  Horses
  Ponies
  Stables
  Competition
  Dressage
  Jumping
  Cross-country
  Showing
ROLE-PLAYING
  Fantasy
ROLLER-BLADING
  No age limit

ROWING
  Join a club
  Row
  Officiate
  Solo
  Pairs
  Fours
  Eights
  Dragon boats
RUGBY
  Union
  League
  Veterans' games
  Coaching
  Refereeing
  Join the club
  Running a team
  Official
  Administrator
SAILBOARDING
  For the fit
SAILING
  Inland
  At sea
  Keeping a boat
  Building a boat
  Competition
  Cruising
SCHOOL
  Become a teacher
  Teaching assistant
  Cook
  Caretaker
  Cleaner

Playground helper
Lollipop person
Volunteer
School governor
Sports teams
Sports day help
Helping with reading
Bringing the past to life
School play
School magazine
Old Boys
Old Girls
SCRAPBOOKS
Any interest
Stars
Local history
Family events
Sport
Theatre
Collections
SCUBA DIVING
Safety first
Searching wrecks
SCULPTURE
Stone
Wood
Scrap metal
Exhibiting
SENIORS NETWORK
Check website
SEWING
Making clothes
Mending clothes
Buttons

SHEEP
Keeping
Lambing
Selling
Competitions
Showing
Breed Societies
SHOOTING
Pistols
Rifles
Competition
Training abroad
Rough shooting
Game birds
SINGING
Anyone can sing
Choirs
Choruses
Directing
Coaching
SKATEBOARDING
A challenge!
SKATING
Ice
Hockey
Roller
Street Hockey
SKIING
Chasing the snow
Off piste
Apre ski
Artificial slopes
Snowboarding

SKILLS
- Make yours pay
- Holiday relief
- Car maintenance
- Valeting
- Driver
- Accounts
- Proof reader
- Film extra
- Researcher
- Telephone sales
- Lecturer
- Teacher
- Examiner
- Delivery service

SNOOKER
- Simple game
- Clubs
- Competitions

SONG
- Anyone can sing
- Choirs and choruses
- Directing
- Coaching

SPORT ENGLAND (GET ACTIVE)
- Check website

SQUASH
- Keep it up

ST JOHN AMBULANCE
- Learn
- Teach
- Attend events

STATELY HOMES
- Visit
- Photograph
- History

STEAM FAIRS
- Attend
- Help
- Maintain
- Rebuild

STEAM RAILWAYS
- Volunteers needed
- Train driver
- Engineer
- Guard
- Tickets

SUB AQUA
- Learn
- Equipment
- Safety

SUDOKU
- Craze here to stay

SURFING
- Have fun in the shallows

SWIMMING
- Health
- Fitness
- Safety
- Social
- Competition
- Pools
- Rivers
- Lakes
- Sea
- Diving

Wet suits
Water polo
Swim the Channel
Clubs
Coaching
Help the next generation
TABLE TENNIS
Skill & guile
TAPESTRY
All sizes
TATOOS
If you really want to
Henna tattoos
TELEVISION
The digital revolution
Dish and/or set-top box
Watch what/when you
want
Videos – hire/buy
Big screen
Competitions
Vote in shows
Text your comments
Send in videos
Free audience tickets
TENNIS
Indoor
Outdoor
Good for socialising
Encourage the kids
Tournaments
Wimbledon
TERRITORIAL ARMY
Weekends

Time off
Real soldiering
Learn skills
Discipline
Obeying orders
Giving orders
Comradeship
THEATRE
Live performances
TOWN COUNCILS
Meetings
Members
Petitions
Formation
TRAINS
Travel the world
Visit
Train spotting
TRAMS
Old/new services
First/last journeys
TRAVEL
Do your own thing
Travel with a purpose
Activity trips
History
Architecture
Package tours
TRUSTS
Helping
Working
Organising
Fund raising
Sponsored events

UNIVERSITY OF THE 3rd AGE
  Check website
VETERAN CARS
  Collecting
  Restoring
  Showing
  Associations
VIDEOS
  Recording family
  Visits/holidays
  Editing
  Sound tracks
  Voice-overs
  Captions
  Do interviews
  Make a film
VINTAGE CARS
  Collecting
  Restoring
  Showing
  Associations
VOLLEYBALL
  Coach
  Official
WALKING
  Best exercise
  Cheap
  Round the block
  Over the hills
  Very sociable
  Walking holidays
  Healthy
  See the country
  Visit places
  Read maps
WAR GAMES
  Choose your war
  Your battle
  Your regiment
  Be a general
  Re-fight old battles
  Take on the greats
  Re-enact history
  Change the result
  Club
  Competitions
  Make miniatures
WEDDINGS
  Supply a service
  Make dresses
  Photographer
  Video maker
WHISKEY
  Drink it
  Keep it
  Visit distilleries
WILD FLOWERS
  Alpine plants
  Pot plants
  Rock gardens
WIND SURFING
  Must be fit
WINE
  Drink it
  Keep it
  See where it's made
  Tasting

Make your own
WOMENS' INSTITUTES
  Up to date
  Social
  Issues
WORK
  Full-time
  Part-time
  Start new business
  Step down
  Reduce stress
  Be a consultant
  Combine work/travel
  Be self-employed
  Start your own business
  Go into business
  Find a new business
    associate
  Work at home
  Night manager
  Make your hobby pay
WORK OUT AT HOME
  Books/Videos
  Home equipment
  Set up your stereo
WRITE
  There's a book in you!
  Hobby
  Business
  Your life story
  Novel
  Poetry
  Local history
  Scripts for radio

  Scripts for tv
  Scripts for film
  Submit jokes/gags
  Get published
  Find a publisher
  Find an agent
  Self-publish
  Magazine articles
  Local correspondent
  Community newsletter
YOGA
  Join a class
YOUTH HOSTELLING
  Join YHA
  Cheap accommodation
  Good facilities
  Country
  Town
  All ages

USEFUL CONTACTS

This information is given in good faith but without any guarantees as to accuracy. Details can always change, so do check.

National Associations

NATIONAL PENSIONERS CONVENTION
www.npcuk.org
19-23 Ironmonger Row, London EC1V 3QP Tel: 0207 553 6510
Britain's biggest pensioner organisation. Seminars, workshops, conferences, rallies. Organises annual Pensioners' Parliament. Lots and lots of useful links.

THE PENSIONERS' PARTY www.pensionersparty.org
109 Coalway Road, Wolverhampton WV3 7NA

OCCUPATIONAL PENSIONERS ALLIANCE
www.opalliance.org.uk
Tel: 01582 663 880

RAMBLERS ASSOCIATION www.ramblers.org.uk
87-90 Albert Embankment, London SE1 7TW Tel: 0207 339 8500
Get walking!

HELLS GERIATRICS www.hellsgeriatrics.co.uk
Grow old disgracefully.

National Charities

HELP THE AGED www.helptheaged.org.uk
207 Pentonville Road, London N1 9UZ
"How to thrive past 55"

AGE CONCERN www.ageconcern.org
Astral House 1268 London Road, London SW16 4ER Tel: 0208 765 7200
Information & advice, insurance, inter-generational projects, volunteers.

ROYAL BRITISH LEGION www.britishlegion.org.uk
Tel: 0845 725 725

BRITISH RED CROSS www.redcross.org.uk
44 Moorside London EC2Y 9AL Tel: 0870 170 7000

CONTACT THE ELDERLY www.contact-the-elderly.org
National charity. Brings older, isolated people together for "cakes and company."

CRUSE BEREAVEMENT CARE
 www.crusebereavementcare.org.uk
126 Sheen Road Richmond Surrey TW9 1UR Tel: 0870 167 1677

ST JOHN AMBULANCE www.sja.org.uk
27 St John's Lane London EC1M 4BU Tel: 08700 10 49 50

UNIVERSAL BENEFICENT SOCIETY www.u-b-s.org.uk
6 Avonmore Road, London W14 8RL Tel: 0207 605 4263
National charity to help over-65s on low incomes.

Magazines

SAGA MAGAZINE www.saga.co.uk/magazine
Embrooke Park, Folkestone Kent CT20 3SE

OLDIE MAGAZINE www.theoldie.co.uk

MATURE TYMES www.maturetymes.co.uk
On-line magazine

AGE-NET www.age-net.co.uk
112 Mewstone Avenue, Wembury, Plymouth PL9 0HT Tel:
01752 862 558
On-line magazine

BRITISH MENSA LTD www.mensa.org.uk
St John's House, St John's Square, Wolverhampton WV2
4AH Tel: 01902 772 771
No age limit! Monthly magazine for members.

On Line

I DON'T FEEL 50 www.idf50.co.uk
Online discussion forum, plus links to relevant job websites
& organizations.

MY PRIME www.myprime.co.uk
Over-50s portal

SENIORITY www.seniority.co.uk
On-line community. Over-50s advertising.

GREYS ON LINE www.greysonline.com
On-line saleroom auction.

SILVER LINKS www.sylviamilne.co.uk

SILVER HAIRS www.silverhairs.co.uk
Silver surfers.

Learning

UNIVERSITY OF THE THIRD AGE www.u3a.com
19 East Street, Bromley, Kent BR1 1QH Tel:0208 466 6139
A co-operative sharing educational, creative and leisure
activities, with groups nationwide.

LIFELONG LEARNING www.lifelonglearning.co.uk
Government-supported, promotion & development.

THE OPEN UNIVERSITY www.open.ac.uk
PO Box 197 Milton Keynes MK7 6BJ Tel: 0845 300 6090
Study at home, meet other late learners.

PROMOTING ADULT LEARNING www.niace.org.uk
Renaissance House, 20 Princess Road West, Leicester LE1
6TP Tel: 0116 204 4200/1
ACTIVE AGE www.activeage.org.uk

THE DARK HORSE VENTURE
www.darkhorse.rapid.co.uk
Encourages over-55 year-olds to discover hidden talents.

Work

NEW DEAL 50 PLUS www.jobcentreplus.gov.uk

WISE OWLS www.wiseowls.co.uk
Unit 7, St Margaret's House, 15 Old Ford Road, London E2
9PJ Tel: 0208 983 9716
Voice of the over-45s. Access to free online learning
packages & recruitment.

FIFTY ON www.fiftyon.co.uk
Work-life balance

Campaigning

UNISON PENSIONS CAMPAIGN
www.unison.uk/pensions
1 Mabledon Place London WC1H 9AJ Tel: 0845 355 0845

PUBLIC & COMMERCIAL SERVICES UNION
www.pcs.org.uk
160 Falcon Street London SW11 2LN Tel: 0207 924 1847
Associate members "Retired but not Retiring"

ASSOCIATION OF RETIRED PENSIONERS
www.arp.org.uk
Medication, Viagra, drugs, jobs, dating.

OCCUPATIONAL PENSIONERS www.opas.org.uk

PENSIONER POWER www.pensionerpower.org.uk
British pensioners.

Help & support

ACTION FOR BLIND PEOPLE
www.actionforblindpeople.org.uk
Support & advice on employment, legal & housing issues.

CARE DIRECTIONS www.caredirections.co.uk
Care help tips.

COMMISSION FOR EQUALITY & HUMAN RIGHTS
www.cehr.org.uk
Kingsgate House 66-74 Victoria Street London SW1E 6SW
Tel: 0207 215 8415

MENOPAUSE MATTERS www.menopausematters.co.uk
Up-to-date information on menopause and health.

Research

CENTRE FOR POLICY ON AGEING www.cpa.org.uk
25-31 Ironmonger Row, London EC1V 3QP Tel: 0207 553 6500

BRITISH SOCIETY FOR RESEARCH ON AGEING
www.bsra.org.uk

NOVARTIS FOUNDATION FOR GERONTOLOGY
www.healthandage.com
Education & innovation

QUALITY IN AGEING www.pavpub.com
Tel: 01273 62322
Quarterly journal, Pavilion Publishing of Brighton.

WORKING WITH OLDER PEOPLE www.pavpub.com
Tel: 01273 62322
Quarterly journal, Pavilion Publishing of Brighton.

Grandparents

GRANDPARENTS ASSOCIATION www.grandparents-association.org.uk
Tel: 0845 434 9585

GRANDPARENTS FEDERATION www.grandparents-federation.org.uk

GRANDPARENTS ACTION GROUP UK
www.daric.co.uk/gagindex.htm

GRANDPARENTS APART www.grandparentsapart.co.uk
Tel: 0141 882 5658
Self-help group to ease the suffering of grandparents, grandchildren & extended families torn apart.

GRANDPARENTS PLUS www.grandparentsplus.org.uk

Advice & services

ARE YOU OVER 50? www.over50.gov.uk
Practical advice on Government support & services.

OLDER PEOPLE'S INFORMATION NETWORK
www.opinorg.uk

50 CONNECT www.50connect.co.uk
Over-50s website

AGE-NET www.age-net.co.uk
Over-50s

SENIORS NETWORK www.seniorsnetwork.co.uk

INDEPENDENT AGE www.independentage.org.uk
6 Avonmore Road, London W14 8RL Tel: 0207 605 4200
Advice for those on low incomes

PENSIONS SERVICE www.thepensionsservice.gov.uk
Government information & advice.

OCCUPATIONAL PENSIONS ADVISORY SERVICE
www.pensionsadvisoryservice.org.uk
Tel: 0845 601 2923

PENSIONS OMBUDSMAN www.pensions-
ombudsman.org.uk
11 Belgrave Road, London SW1V 1RB Tel: 0207 834 9144

SCOTTISH PARLIAMENT www.scottish.parliament.uk
Tel: 0131 348 5000; 0845 278 1999

AGE CONCERN CYMRU (WALES) www.accymru.org.uk

CONTACT THE ELDERLY WALES
www.beehive.thisissouthwales.co.uk
PO Box 76, Penarth, Wales CF64 4XN Tel: 02920 514 996
Monthly outing & afternoon tea to relieve the isolation of
housebound elderly people.

WELSH ASSEMBLY www.wales.gov.uk

NORTHERN IRELAND ASSEMBLY
www.niassembly.gov.uk

AGE ACTION IRELAND www.ageaction.ie
A network of organisations and individuals for older people.

SPORT

Remember, there is always a role for you in coaching/admin/judging/refereeing even if you are unable to take part yourself.

SPORT ENGLAND (GET ACTIVE)
www.sportengland.org/index/get_active.htm
3rd Floor, Victoria House, Bloomsbury, London WC1B 4se
Tel: 08458 508 508
1,500 locations to play sport, get fit & have fun!

AMATEUR SWIMMING ASSOCIATION
www.britishswimming.org
Harold Fern House, Derby Square, Loughborough, Leics
LE11 5AL Tel: 01509 618 700

ATHLETICS www.ukathletics.net
Athletics House, Central Boulevard Blythe Valley Park, Solihull, West Midlands B90 8AJ

BADMINTON www.badminton.co.uk
National Badminton Centre, Milton Keynes MK8 9LA Tel: 01908 268 412

BOXING www.aba.co.uk

BRIDGE www.ebu.co.uk
English Bridge Union, Broadfields, Bicester Road, Aylesbury HP19 8AZ Tel: 01296 317200

BRITISH DEAF SPORTS COUNCIL
www.britishdeafsportscouncil.org.uk
49 Fonnerau Road, Ipswich IP1 3JN Tel: 01268 510 621

CANOEING www.bcu.org.uk
British Canoe Union, John Dudderidge House, Adbolton
Lane, West Bridgford, Nottingham NG2 5AS

CRICKET www.ecb.co.uk

CYCLISTS TOURING CLUB www.ctc.org.uk
PO Box 510, Unit 8, Fleming Way, Isleworth TW7 6WP Tel:
0870 873 0061
Britain's largest cycling organisation.

ENGLISH AMATEUR DANCESPORT ASSOCIATION
www.eada.org.uk
PO Box 7348 Hook RG27 7EA

FOOTBALL ASSOCIATION www.thefa.com

GLIDING www.gliding.co.uk
British Gliding Association, Kimberley House, Vaughan
Way, Leicester LE1 4SE

GRAND NATIONAL ARCHERY SOCIETY www.gnas.org
Lilleshall National Sports Centre, nr Newport, Shropshire
TF10 9AT Tel: 01952 606 019

HANG GLIDING & PARAGLIDING www.bhpa.co.uk
The Old Schoolroom, Loughborough, Leics LE4 5PJ Tel:
0116 261 1322
Learn to fly!

HOCKEY www.englandhockey.co.uk
The National Hockey Stadium, Silbury Boulevard, Milton
Keynes MK 9 1HA Tel: 01908 544 644

HORSE RIDING www.bhs.org.uk
British Horse Society, Stoneleigh Deer Park, Kenilwort,
Warwicks CV8 2XZ Tel: 08701 202244

IRISH SPORTS COUNCIL www.irishsportscouncil.ie

NATIONAL CYCLING CENTRE
www.britishcycling.org.uk
Stuart Street, Manchester M11 4DQ Tel: 0870 871 2000

NATIONAL ICE SKATING ASSOCIATION
www.iceskating.org.uk
National Ice Centre, Lower Parliament Street, Nottingham
NG1 1LA

NETBALL www.england-netball.co.uk
9 Paynes Park, Hitchin, Herts SG5 1EH Tel: 01462 442 344

NORTHERN IRELAND SPORTS COUNCIL
www.sportni.net
House of Sport, Upper Malone Road, Belfast BT9 5LD

ORIENTEERING www.british orienteering.org.uk
8A Standcliffe House, Whitworth Road, Darley Dale,
Matlock, Derbys DE4 2HJ Tel: 01629 734 042

ROWING www.ara-rowing.org
Amateur Rowing Association

RUGBY UNION www.rfu.com

RUGBY LEAGUE (AMATEUR) www.barla.org.uk
West Yorkshire House, 4 New North Road Parade,
Huddersfield HD1 5JP tel: 01481 544 131

SAILING www.uksail.com
English Institute of Sport, Sheffield S9 5DA Tel: 0114 223
5654

SQUASH www.squash.org
World Squash Federation, 6 Havelock Road, Hastings, East
Sussex TN34 1BP
SCOTTISH ARCHERY www.scottisharchery.org.uk

SPORT SCOTLAND www.sportscotland.org.uk
Caledonia House, South Gyle, Edinburgh EH12 9DQ Tel:
0131 317 7200

SPORTS COUNCIL FOR WALES www.sports-council-
wales.co.uk
Sophia Gardens, Cardiff CF11 9SW Tel: 0845 0904

TABLE TENNIS www.englishtabletennis.org.uk

TENNIS www.lta.org.uk
Lawn Tennis Association, Palliser Road, West Kensington,
London W14 9EG Tel: 0207 381 7000

TRIATHLON www.britishtriathlon.org
PO Box 25, Loughborough, Leics LE11 3WX Tel: 01509 226
161

VETERANS CYCLING (TIME TRIALLING)
www.vtta.org.uk
Tel: 01772 813335

INDEX

Chapter Five
1. Daily Telegraph 10.06.06
2. Times 21.12.06
3. Daily Telegraph 9.12.04
4. Northern Echo 03.02.07
5. Sun 31.12.04
6. Times 23.12.04
7. Northern Echo 24.12.04
8. Daily Telegraph 29.05.06
9. Newcastle Journal
   11.05.06
10. Manchester Evening
    News 26.04.06
11. Daily Telegraph
    11.09.06
12. Northern Echo 02.02.07
13. Sunday Times 28.01.07

Chapter Six
1. Daily Telegraph 13.9.05
2. Daily Telegraph 02.02.07
3. Sunday Sun 26.12.04
4. Times 07.02.06
5. Daily Telegraph 14.02.05
6. Sunday Times 22.10.06
7. Private Eye 31.03.06
8. various 2006
9. Durham Advertiser
   29.06.06
10. Times 06.03.06
11. Durham Advertiser
    16.11.06

Chapter Seven
1. Daily Telegraph 25.07.06
2. Daily Telegraph 11.10.06
3. Durham Advertiser
   09.11.06
4. Times 03.01.07
5. Northern Echo 01.02.05
6. Daily Telegraph 11.10.06
7. Journal 09.12.06
8. Northern Echo 15.02.07

Chapter Eight
1. Times 02.01.07
2. Times 26.11.06

Chapter Nine
1. Daily Telegraph 12.02.07
2. Times 31.12.04
3. Times 07.12.04.
4. Sunday Sun 12.12.04
5. Daily Telegraph 02.02.05
6. Times of India/Sunday
   Times 13.08.06
7. Times 19.07.06
8. Sunday Times 07.05.06
9. Times 07.04.06
10. Sunday Times 02.04.06
11. Sunday Times 26.03.06
12. Daily Telegraph
    07.02.06
13. Daily Telegraph
    12.12.06

14. Sunday Times 31.12.06
15. Sunday Times 16.01.05
16. Daily Telegraph
    25.04.06
17. Daily Telegraph
    03.10.05
18. Sunday Times 28.01.07
19. Times 03.06.06
20. Daily Telegraph
    16.12.05

Chapter Ten
1. Daily Telegraph 07.02.05
2. Sunday Times 14.01.07

Chapter Eleven
1. Daily Telegraph 23.01.07
2. Sunday Times 18.06.06

Chapter Twelve
1. Times 08.02.06
2. Times 14.09.05
3. Times 09.10.06
4. Daily Telegraph 19.05.06
5. Sun 28.12.04
6. Northern Echo January
   2007
7. Newcastle Journal
   26.1.05
8. Northern Echo 03.01.05

Chapter Thirteen
1. Sunday Sun 09.01.05
2. Daily Telegraph 15.08.06
3. Times 02.10.05

Chapter Fourteen
1. Northern Echo 14.08.06
2. Sunday Times 18.12.05
3. Daily Telegraph 13.12.05
4. Daily Mirror 09.12.05
5. Daily Telegraph 30.08.06
6. Sunday Times 22.10.06
7. Times 11.12.06
8. Daily Telegraph 22.12.06
9. Times 21.01.06

ABOUT THE AUTHOR

Chris Foote Wood was born in Prestbury, Cheshire in December 1940, the first of four children of Helen and Stanley Wood from Manchester. The Woods settled in Bury, Lancashire. Chris's youngest sister, the comedienne, writer and comic actor Victoria Wood, has several times been voted the UK's funniest woman. Their late father Stanley was a successful author and playwright.

Chris was a scholarship boy at Bury Grammar School, 1950-59. He won an open scholarship to Manchester University, but instead took a BSc honours degree course in civil engineering at King's College, Newcastle upon Tyne, then part of Durham University, 1959-62. Chris completed the course but was not awarded a degree.

After various civil engineering jobs, including a spell as bridge engineer on the A1(M) Durham motorway construction, in 1968 Chris set up his own publishing business, Durham Free Press, pioneering local free press newspapers in the UK. He gave up the venture in 1971 and had one further civil engineering job on the A19 Teesside construction for four years, before returning to journalism as a freelance writer and broadcaster. In 1974 Chris set up his own regional press agency, North Press News & Sport, and ran it for thirty years. He sold NPA in 2004 and is now a full-time freelance writer and publisher.

Chris wrote his first weekly newspaper column at the age of sixteen, reporting athletics for the *Bury Times*. He wrote for his college newspaper *"Courier"*. He edited and promoted the student arts magazine *"Northerner"*, making it profitable for the first (and perhaps the only) time. As well as publishing and editing his own local newspapers in the north east, Chris has written and published books of local interest. *"Nellie's Book"*, published by Sutton Publishing in February 2006, was his first venture onto the national scene. He now specialises in biography and is an accomplished "ghost writer."

As a boy, Chris suffered TB on the lungs which prevented any sporting activity for three years, up to the age of sixteen. He then took up athletics and cross-country running, winning his school's top sportsman award and representing Northern Schools in the mile. He also competed for the school chess team. Chris won many form prizes and was awarded the school's senior mathematics prize. Chris took up marathon running at the age of forty, and he still competes regularly in veteran athletics, cycling, and the triathlon.

From the age of ten, Chris has been a keen participant in amateur dramatics and pantomime. As an adult, he has appeared in many productions for the Bishop Auckland Little Theatre company, and in other shows. In his work as a news and sports reporter, Chris has made hundreds of broadcasts on local and national radio.

Chris Wood married Frances Foote (now OBE) in 1977, adding her surname to his by deed poll. They have no children, but Chris has three children from his first marriage and two grandchildren.

April 2007

Other books by Chris Foote Wood

"Baghdad Trucker" (Northern Writers 2006)
The true-life adventures of a long-distance truck driver
who helped pioneer the overland route to the Middle East
on "the most dangerous roads in the world." As co-author,
with Kevin Noble.

"Nellie's Book – The Early Life of Victoria Wood's Mother"
Foreword by Victoria Wood. (Sutton Publishing 2006).
Surviving poverty in industrial Manchester in the 1920s
and 1930s. Helen Colleen (Nellie) Mape, born 1919, was
one of eight children born to very poor Irish Catholic
parents. Nellie worked full-time at a steelworks from the
age of fourteen, met her husband Stanley Wood at
eighteen, and by the end of WW2 was married with two
children. *"Nellie's Book"* is the remarkably detailed story of
a girl growing up in real poverty, telling how her large
working-class family managed to stay above the breadline.
Based on her notes and essays – in later life Nellie gained
a BA degree and an MA. She died in 2001, with her
writings largely unpublished. This is her story, largely in
Nellie's own words.

"Land of The 100 Quangos" (North Press 2002)
An expose of the 100-plus appointed and largely unknown
government-funded organisations who run the North East.

"Kings of Amateur Soccer" (North Press 1985)
The official centenary history of Bishop Auckland Football
Club, ten times FA Amateur Cup winners and the most
famous and successful amateur soccer club of all time.

"BISHOP AUCKLAND IN OLD PICTURE POSTCARDS"
(European Library 1985).
Local history in words and pictures.

All these books are available on Ebay, Amazon and on Chris's website www.northernwriters.co.uk

Other titles published by Capall Bann

Gardening For Wildlife   by Ron Wilson

"If you have only one wildlife book, this is the one to have. The information contained in this book is invaluable. A very interesting read for young and old alike, to which you will always refer." The Professional Gardener   "..*a real delight...a fascinating read...all of the methods I have tried so far have gleaned superb results***" Touchstone   "lively, colloquial style...quick and easy to read...inspiring and full of helpful tips'** Place

"..a nice book...lively drawings which clearly illustrate techniques...covers everything...a good starter book" Permaculture

A few 'modifications' and additions could enhance the value of most gardens for wildlife. That is what this book is all about. It offers practical advice and ideas for improvements and where possible suggests the inclusion of 'extra' features which will support and encourage a rich diversity of plant, insect, bird and animal life. Plants, foods and features are all described in plain English. Everything in this book is explained in straightforward terms to enable anyone to help their local wildlife. ISBN 1 86163 011 5   £10.95

The Transformation of Housework   by Ben Bushill

Do you ever find the never-ending stream of jobs around the house a trial, time to be resented, rather than used and enjoyed? *The Transformation of Housework* shows you how to bring a new lightness and energy to those chores. How to use the time we must spend doing housework in a more creative and positive way. By connecting the principles of Tai-chi and meditation to everyday actions the reader is able to experience the benefits of these practices in a very real and down to earth way. Simple exercises, cartoons and photographs show you how to connect to the chi energy and how to bring that energy into your chores and your life. Photographs show some basic Tai-chi movements and principles and how these can be applied to our household jobs. It is a way of teaching those of us with hectic, stressed lives to slow down and find a little space for ourselves in the midst of the chaos, a reminder to look at the world a little differently and blow a big raspberry at the mind that thinks it knows everything there is to know about washing the dishes. *The Transformation of Housework* will show you some surprises in those things you thought you knew. The whole book is presented in a light-hearted way, never taking itself too seriously and inviting people to laugh at themselves and the fact that they've "got to do the damn housework" yet again. This is a fun-filled book that also contains real learning - it will revolutionise your relationship with your housework!   ISBN 186163 1820   £8.95

The Way the Cookie Crumbles   by Malcolm Kidd
"...source of considerable interest.... lively confessions.... strong thread of humour.... hearty laughter inspired by minor misfortunes and amiable eccentricities." The Keswick Reminder

Introducing himself as a "mail order cattle salesman" - in addition to farming, Malcolm Kidd has had a full and colourful life, meeting 'worthies' and rogues in abundance. He describes his boyhood on the farm, and six wartime years in the army where he managed to start at the top and work his way down! Country tales of local squires, gamekeepers and poachers are nostalgic and often humourous. The book is illustrated with numerous period photographs.
ISBN 186163 1529£10.95

Can't Sleep, Won't Sleep - Insomnia, Reasons and Remedies
by Linda Louisa Dell

This book gives some of the many reasons for sleep problems and sets out some of the many remedies, therapies and techniques that can help you to re-train your sleep patterns to your very individual needs. Starting with an explanation of what insomnia is, the author progresses to cover the purposes of sleep, dreaming, sleep posture, depression, chronic fatigue, women's problems, stress, SAD, relaxation techniques, hands-on healing, and much much more. Problems and possible remedies are blended here making fascinating reading and a real help for anyone experiencing sleep problems - and so many of us have for all sorts of reasons. Help yourself get a good night's sleep - read this!
ISBN 186163 238X   £13.95

In Pursuit of Perennial Profit - The Pot of Gold at the Bottom of the Garden   by Patrick Vickery

Shows how to make your garden productive in a variety of ways, for both expert and gardening novice alike, at minimum cost and in an innovative and self-financing way. For those who know little or nothing about gardening this will start you on your way - a journey of discovery and self-fulfilment. Choosing plants to grow, organising time and space (you don't need much of either!), deterring slugs, getting the best from the plants and even how to sell excess plants should you wish are all covered here. The author writes from real experience, growing plants in the not always ideal location of Ross-shire in Scotland, as he says ""if I can do it, anybody can".
ISBN 186163 1480   £7.95

Crowning Disasters by Yeoman Warder Geoffrey Abbott

As a member of the Queen's Bodyguard of the Yeoman of the Guard Extraordinary (Beefeater) Geoffrey Abbott is well qualified to write books on strange happenings at regal events. The topics covered in this fascinating book range from the hilarious to the unlikely and in some cases quite macabre. Contents include: Things that went wrong at coronations; OMENS AND AUGURIES when disasters occurred during a monarch's reign, FEASTS AND AFFRAYS coronation banquets which frequently ended in chaos, riots and looting; table manners of the day; royal menus; Coronation robes and their ultimate fate - sold; given to Mme Tussaud's; used in plays; SLEAZE FOR SYCOPHANTS perks for parasites, favours for flatterers, titles for toadies; PALACE PASTIMES flirting and wooing, masques and mistresses, dice-playing, jesters, and other right royal entertainments; ROYAL ODDITIES regal pretenders and their fate; the English queen tried for witchcraft; coronation medals; duties of the Yeomen of the Guard; Royal letters; attempted assassinations; Napoleon Bonaparte once a London Special Constable!
ISBN 186163 1324   £10.95

Regalia, Robbers and Royal Corpses by Yeoman Warder Geoffrey Abbott

Anyone with even the vaguest interest in tradition will be fascinated, amused and in some cases shocked by the incredible facts disclosed here. Contents include: GEMS AND THEIR JOURNEYS the magical world of coronation jewels, the peacock throne, Koh-i-Nur, Star of Africa, Moon of the Mountains; their origins and travels; owners tortured to hand them over; diamond dust used as poison. "STOP THIEF!" stories behind famous jewel thefts; the missing Irish regalia; Colonel Blood and the Crown Jewels; the gem found in the stomach of the slain messenger who had swallowed it when attacked; this nation's treasures stolen by Westminster monks. CORPSES, COFFINS AND CONTENTS when royal coffins were opened centuries later, some contained no heads, others too many; crowns and jewels had been stolen. Who stole Richard II's jawbone? Eastern tombs plundered : the craft of mummification. ISBN 186163 1316   £9.95

Contact: Capall Bann Publishing, Auton Farm, Milverton, Somerset, TA4 1NE
Tel 01823 401528   www.capallbann.co.uk
email: enquiries@capallbann.co.uk